THE PAPER ARK

THE PAPER ARK

BY

BILL CLARK

ILLUSTRATIONS BY

ERIC MACHÉ

*E*VEREST HOUSE
Publishers   *New York*

DEDICATION

FOR EVERY ANIMAL taken from the cages of a zoo to be
released in the wilderness where it belongs, and for
the young of these animals that symbolize the
greatest hope of wildlife restoration. And especially
for the Arabian oryx born at the Hai Bar South
Reserve in the fall of 1978—the first of its kind born
in the Holy Land in nearly a millennium.

Text Copyright © 1979 by Bill Clark
Illustrations Copyright © 1979 by Eric Maché
All Rights Reserved
Library of Congress Catalog Card Number: 78–65531
ISBN: 0–89696–033–1
Published simultaneously in Canada by
Beaverbooks, Pickering, Ontario
Manufactured in the United States of America
Printed by Reehl Litho, New York City, N.Y.
Bound by American Book–Stratford Press, Inc., Saddle Brook, N.J.
Designed by Sam Gantt
First Edition

CONTENTS

ACKNOWLEDGMENTS

I MUST THANK, for the incalculable advice, suggestions, assistance, and encouragement so freely offered me during the preparation of this book, the good offices of the Israeli Nature Reserve Authority, particularly its director, General Avraham Yoffe, and his several reserve area wardens, especially Mr. Michael van Greven Grock, chief warden of the Hai Bar South reserve; also, the staffs of the Rockefeller Museum and Israel Museum, the Jerusalem Biblical Zoo and Tel Aviv Zoo, as well as the many individuals whose scholarship and common sense have been invaluable in the research for this book.

Special thanks to Ms. Esther Lurie, my mother-in-law, who wouldn't let me go into the desert without a nourishing breakfast, a box lunch, and a proper hat. And to my wife Judy for supporting my work and dreams. And to my son Joe, who learned to tell an addax from an ibex before he was three.

A special acknowledgment is made to Cleo Crouch, for his understanding and generous support of the project, as well as to the Holy Land Conservation Fund and its coordinator, Mr. Gilbert Jones, who first whetted my interest in the unique beauties of scriptural fauna.

And finally, thanks to Ms. Alice Herrington of Friends of Animals, whose wisdom and common sense understanding of man's relations and responsibilities toward non-human species is a continuing source of enlightenment for me.

A portion of the profits made by this book will be presented to the Holy Land Conservation Fund to assist in their continuing efforts to preserve endangered species mentioned in Holy Scripture.

PREFACE

". . . in wisdom hast thou made them all!" (PSALMS 104:24)

A SENSE of wonder pervades Scripture. The world of sacred writings is a world of enchantment which, despite its roots in an ancient and remote past, is one of the brightest illuminations for our contemporary world.

A magnificent collection of profound thought is to be found in Scripture. It ranges from the deepest abstractions of divine inspiration to the simple clarity of human morality. The "Good Book," whether considered in Judaic, Christian, or Islamic context, is a volume of wealth for the philosopher and common man alike.

An integral and essential part of Scripture is fauna. The animal life that exists so abundantly through thousands of verses of sacred writing fulfills critical functions, serving to reveal the meaning of the holy word. The better we understand what these animals are, and what their particular character-istics are, the better we understand the meaning of Scripture itself.

This is no easy task. The Scriptures of man's monotheistic religions were written tens of centuries ago, at a time when man was much closer to the earth. Ancient man lived at a time when humanity was bound ever so closely to both the domestic and wild animals that shared his land. Ancient societies knew these animals, their habits, strengths, and frailties much better than modern societies do. Ancient man could color his speech with allusions to particular animals when he described partic-ular characteristics of himself, his fellowman, and his God.

Today, we are far removed from that ancient world. For many of us, the only wildlife we see is a stray cat slinking be-tween parked automobiles or a dozen pigeons pecking crumbs in a neighborhood park. The only connection many of us have with the large beasts, cattle and sheep, is after they have been slaughtered and neatly wrapped in cellophane at the neighborhood market.

Even the minority who have escaped modern urbanization and live in the dwindling rural areas of the world have not escaped the estrangement between man and beast. Our eggs come from climate-controlled hen houses where electric bulbs replace the sun, where chickens are kept in small cells, and most often never set their feet to the earth. Our milk comes from dairies with automatic, electric milking machines, where modern machinery ensures cleanliness, periodic feeding, and even artificial insemination of the bovine.

Wildlife in these rural areas is often looked upon as a nuisance. Predators are hunted down because of their natural instincts. Herbivorous species are exterminated because of supposed threats to man's economy of agriculture. And those species that try their utmost to avoid the human community, fleeing to the most secluded areas, are too frequently hunted for the perverted sport of the chase and glory of the trophy.

Practically, it is a rare instance when an animal is left with its own right to live. Our overpopulated world and insatiable taste for meat have conspired to relegate animal life to a position that is essentially economic. We must ensure that our children have milk, that our families are well fed, that we have woolen sweaters and leather shoes, and even bone meal to fertilize our flower gardens. When all our requirements are met, when the animal has provided its blood for our food, warmth, and pleasure, then a few people turn their attention to the relevance of it all. And this minority of humans is nearly dumbfounded with what man has done to the greatness of Creation.

It is no wonder, then, that when we leaf through a few pages of Scripture we find a completely different world. So often, these sacred writings seem exotic; they become visions cast in an aura of fabulous remoteness. But Scripture isn't fable. Each day, some scholar, or archaeologist, or historian unearths centuries of sand to find a new validity for Scripture. Armageddon is no longer a speculative fancy; it is a real place, found during this century at Tell Megiddo in northern Israel. The once mythical King Solomon's mines are no longer a myth; they are a stark reality that stood lost for centuries deep in the Negev Desert, only to be discovered again less than a half century ago. With deliberate diligence, modern man is finding the reality of Scripture manifest in the physical world.

We are developing substantive proofs of Scripture. We are finding a world that many had accepted on blind faith while others dismissed it as myth. In so doing, we clear the dust of centuries and find a reality of reason and fact in Scripture. Faith in the validity of the sacred writings no longer needs to be blind. We can see clearly the rich truths of those ancient writings. We can touch the walls of Jericho, which fell before Joshua's armies, and stand in the synagogue of Capernaum, where Jesus once preached.

While much progress is being made in the archaeological field to substantiate man's sacred writings, other fields are also being drawn into this amazing investigation of the roots of modern man's religion and morality. And one such field is zoology.

A century ago, scholars could readily identify the goats and sheep so frequently used in scriptural metaphor, but when it came to unicorns, dragons, and behemoths, people were prone to dismiss them as mythical beasts. But today it appears as if these myths are of the same validity as Armageddon and King Solomon's mines. They are being identified with the same assiduity as the ancient walls of Jericho and synagogue of Capernaum. The unicorn, which since the Middle Ages we have shrouded with fantastic myth, today appears to have been a species of antelope that wandered the deserts of the Middle East. It appears to have been the Arabian oryx, a beautiful and rare animal of mostly white color, with two closely spaced horns that are almost perfectly straight. Viewed from a profile, they appear as one.

Zoologists and etymologists have collaborated in identifying the dragons of Scripture. Today there is general agreement that misunderstandings have given a single name to at least two species. There is agreement that the ancient Hebrews knew the jackal as *tan,* or in plural *tannim,* and sea monsters—perhaps the crocodile—as *tannin.* A single, misplaced letter gave this beast the power to wail across a barren desert and churn a river into a frothy mire. For medieval scholars, such an animal could only have been some kind of dragon. Today we know better.

Other misunderstandings are less spectacular, but just as much misidentifications. The medieval translators who put the Bible into English knew little about the wildlife that inhabited the Middle East. Thus, when they came to a species they did not know, they identified it with a species they did know from their European environment. Consequently, the *zvi* that bounded lightly across the Song of Songs became known to English readers of the Bible as a deer. Wrong. Today we know it was a gazelle.

The zoological inquiry continues as the archaeological. Modern man is extracting more and more truths from his sacred writings. The worlds of David, Jesus, and Mohammed are becoming more apparent, and because we are better able to understand their worlds, we are better able to understand their words.

What this all boils down to is simple. We live in an age that scoffs superstition and blind faith. We are pragmatic realists. We are rationalists who demand truth "beyond all reasonable doubt." If the events, places, and observations of Scripture are clouded, if we have no substantial evidence or proof, then all the inspiration and morality founded in these events, places, and observations are cloaked in the same shadow of unreality. The commandments received by Moses, the humane teachings of Christ, and the austere philosophy of Mohammed slip into the abyss of "wishful thinking." Scriptural truth is no longer axiomatic.

But the more we learn of scriptural truth, the more we find it was never meant to be axiomatic. We learn that these truths are founded in proven reality. We learn that there is a simple lucidity to Scripture that was meant to be understood by the great masses of humanity.

The words of Scripture were well understood by the ancients. The finest points were part of their everyday lives. The allusions, images, and metaphors used in Scripture were modes of communication that enhanced understanding. Unfortunately, many of these devices were lost in the passage of centuries, and what was once an obvious simile became a mysterious relationship. It is then quite easy to pass off these mysteries as belonging to the realm of the supernatural. It became accepted that Scripture was written under divine inspiration, and it is not man's prerogative to know the divine. It became accepted that the mysteries of Scripture would be unfolded before us in eternity.

However, whether one believes Scripture was written by either divine or human hand, one cannot contest that it was written for the human mind. God does not need to read his own words fixed in ink on paper. And if the message of Scripture is considered to be of such high significance for man, it is difficult to believe the message would be couched in passages too cryptic for man to understand.

Thus, we must revert to the origins and pick up those original meanings that were lost during ages past. We have much to start with: We have the texts of Scripture and continuous traditions that have carried many themes and ideas intact. We have our own inquisitiveness, coupled with reasonable minds and a growing mass of research.

Concerning scriptural fauna, we have many idioms that stem directly from sacred writings. Why is the lion "king of beasts"? Who conferred this nobility to a brute cat that isn't even the mightiest of the family Felidae? When we call someone a "dog," why is it a name of derogation when we recognize the dog as "man's best friend"? What is it in the character of the stork to which myth entrusts the delivery of infants? All of these, and so many more, are directly linked to Scripture. Animals do not wander into Scripture by chance. Each has a particular characteristic that the author of Scripture is trying to convey to the reader. Each was selected specifically to illustrate a point and each one of these points forms a concept that in varying degrees has shaped, stimulated, and sustained the way of life for the contemporary world.

The scriptural concepts illustrated through animal imagery and metaphor exist outside our synagogues, churches, and mosques as well as inside. They are part of our everyday world. They form illuminating links to vital issues of contemporary politics, economy, and philosophy. And as we uncover the original meanings of these concepts, we are better able to understand the driving forces of our culture and our place in it.

This book is a paper ark. Where Noah used gopher wood to construct an ark to carry the flesh of animals, we are using paper to build a volume to carry the meaning of animals.

The object of the following chapters is simple: to identify and relate peculiar characteristics of the more significant animals in Scripture, and then to knot these characteristics into the scriptural intent for including a particular species.

The identification alone is frequently difficult. It's relatively easy to establish the identity of sheep, horses, and camels. They are domestic beasts that have served man in the Middle East for centuries and are common to this day. But other species require some thinking and some fieldwork. For instance, the "wild goats" mentioned by David in the Psalms can with good certainty be identified with the Nubian ibex, a spectacular animal only recently threatened with extinction. This certainty is found by studying the observations made by David and recorded in the Psalms, by comparing this with archaeological evidence collected in the vicinity of David's exile at the Judean desert oasis of En-gedi, and then by physically climbing the towering cliffs around the oasis to seek out the small herd of ibex and comparing their habits with the archaeological and scriptural evidence.

Some species are more difficult to ascertain. Jewish and Islamic law forbids "graven images." Thus we have no graphic likenesses of many species that existed during the writing of these Scriptures. We must look elsewhere; geology, geography, history, etymology, and a dozen other sciences that may give clues. In some cases, such as the wild ass and ostrich, the evidence seems conclusive; in other cases, such as leviathan and behemoth, our evidence is a bit inconclusive, but still enough to suggest an identity that seems reasonable.

Then there are other species, such as the biblical pygarg, which is open to the broadest speculation. Here, we can offer a tentative identification which must remain open-ended until someone unearths more clues to either confirm or disprove our theories.

With respect for the Scriptures of the three religions that are incorporated in these pages, dates are given as C.E. (common era) and B.C.E. (before the common era), equivalent to the dating system used by the Western world, but eliminating the arbitrary Christian use of "before Christ" and "anno Domini." The common era year 1979 is also 5739 in the Judaic calendar and 1398 in the Islamic.

The characteristics of most animals in this book were recorded from direct observation after researching several zoological authorities. In cases where the species is extinct or extirpated, observations are those garnered from reputable experts alone. In most cases, the first authority is Scripture. It is amazing to note the acute zoological observations made by men such as Job and Isaiah, and many others, centuries before man devised the scientific studies of natural history. Christ knew the distinctive qualities of sheep and fish, and Mohammed knew the attributes of the camel and horses, to exactness, before they could so well include them in the metaphors and observations in the Scriptures of Christianity and Islam.

Also surprising is the number of species mentioned in Scripture that still exist today. It is still possible to find species we know today as addax, oryx, griffon vulture, and onager in the Middle East. Unfortunately, however, our generation may be the last in history to view many of them alive in their natural habitat.

Just as the twentieth century has been responsible for unearthing the physical truth of Scripture, it is also responsible for annihilating many of the species that form the great literary and spiritual genius that is the sacred writings of monotheism. We no sooner have a tentative identification for the unicorn, after centuries of believing the animal to be nonexistent, than we drive this antelope to the brink of extinction. For the next generation, this unicorn/oryx may just as well have never been discovered, for it is quite possible that it will become exterminated and slip back into that shadowy realm of myth.

Many species have already gone this route. The Syrian wild ass, which some traditions claim is the animal Christ used on his Palm Sunday entry into Jerusalem, is extinct in this century. The last of the Syrian ostriches, described in detail by Job, was slaughtered and eaten during World War II. There are other species that have vanished, and man shall never be able to duplicate them.

Lost species are forever gone, and we can do little but lament their extinction. But other species still live, and there is still time, in this generation, to save them if enough resources and energies are mustered for the job.

There are three main reasons why these rare species are on the road to extinction, and all are attributable to man. The first reason is war. For centuries, armies have clashed in the Middle East, but it is only the twentieth century that has devised and used such utterly devastating weapons. It was relatively easy for a dorcas gazelle, one of the rarest and most beautiful in the world, to duck away from a Crusader cavalry charge or a Turkish infantry assault. But it is quite another thing when this gazelle is trapped between two advancing armies that spread thousands of tanks across miles of terrain in their advances. The destructiveness of long-range artillery and lightning air strikes has taken its toll of wildlife. Off-duty soldiers, seeking fresh meat to supplement their rations, have been known to train their automatic weapons on the dwindling desert species and further cut into their small numbers.

The second reason for pending extinctions is hunting. The jet age has equipped the sophisticated hunter with everything he needs to obtain an extremely rare trophy for his wall.

The Middle East can be reached from anywhere in the world, comfortably, within a day. Once on the scene, small aircraft can be rented, the hunter outfitted with a long-range, telescopic-sighted rifle, and guides retained to point out the last remaining grounds of the endangered species. The hunt can be carried out in a few hours, and the hunter need not bother getting his shoes dusty.

Personnel manning the oil fields in desolate locales also contribute to the carnage. Understandably, their work areas do not have much to offer in the way of diversion during leisure time. But not understandably, they throw a few rifles in their all-terrain vehicles and set off for a hunt.

So ended the last wild herds of the Arabian oryx—the "unicorn" to Bible readers. The last of these magnificent creatures was killed by hunters in the Arabian desert in 1972. Fortunately, some farsighted conservationists saw the end coming and had the wisdom to start a captive breeding program which rescued the species in the eleventh hour.

The third reason is habitat destruction—man's recent explosions of population and technology have made serious incursions into the habitats of the most remote and forbidding areas of the Middle East. The quest for human living space, agriculture, and oil has deprived much wildlife of its traditional habitat.

There are other bright spots too. The Nubian ibex's recovery from near extinction is one of the more notable successes. Had the proper care not been taken by serious conservationists a mere decade ago, the Nubian ibex might well be extinct today. Most of the groundwork and planning for the rescue was the work of Avraham Yoffe, a retired Israeli general who made his reputation, ironically, on the battlefield. He is best known for his swift, strategic capture of Mitla Pass in Sinai during the Six-day War. Unlike most other generals, Israeli and Arab alike, Yoffe had conservation matters floating in the back of his mind even during the heat of battle.

While his own troops were still engaged in fierce battles, Yoffe dug into his supplies, pulled out Nature Reserves Authority markers, and ordered some reserve troops to post them at specified areas he noticed that would make valuable nature reserves. Before the guns had stopped in that brief war, thousands of acres of Sinai had been posted and to this day are inviolate sanctuaries for desert wildlife.

Working with an annual budget equal to what the state of New York spends on conservation in two weeks, Yoffe has built one of the most remarkable nature reserve systems in the Middle East. He is assisted by the Hai Bar Society, an Israeli conservation group that has made commendable efforts toward the preservation of endangered species in their country.

The Holy Land Conservation Fund, an American organization, is also involved in the wildlife preservation effort. In 1972, when the fund was first organized, the group set a goal of rescuing seven endangered species that are mentioned in Scripture. With the arrival of eight Arabian oryx in a Negev reserve last year, they have achieved their goal. Thanks to this group's efforts, the only captive breeding herd of Somali wild ass is now secure in the Negev. The largest captive breeding herds of the Nubian ibex, the Persian onager, and the dorcas gazelle are there also. Breeding herds of Ethiopian ostrich, addax, Scimitar-horned (Sahara) and Arabian oryx complete the population.

For most of these species, this final effort of captive breeding is the last chance they have for survival. It is the last chance for these animals we read about in the pages of Job and Isaiah, in Matthew and Luke, and in the many Surahs of the Koran.

The Israeli conservation effort also represents the seed for starting better wildlife protection practices through the entire Middle East, as well as offering a nonpolitical ground for Jews and Arabs to work together on. In the Sinai, Yoffe has trained several Arabs to tend the reserve areas there, with the hope that once the desert tract is returned to Egypt, there will be a nucleus of trained conservationists to continue work under Egyptian rule. Likewise, the Holy Land Conservation Fund has made overtures to various Arab governments, seeking to assist them in starting nature reserve areas for the protection of scriptural fauna. The administration of the fund realizes that the term "Holy Land" encompasses more than Israel, extending from the torrid Egyptian Nile delta to the arid deserts near Mecca. The biblical kingdoms of Edom and Moab are now in territory administered by Jordan, and the kingdom of Phoenecia is now part of Lebanon.

There is no such thing as a Jewish ibex, or a Christian onager, or an Islamic camel. All are part of a rich scriptural culture that has served humanity far beyond the borders of the Middle East. It is critical that concern for these animals be considered a nondenominational effort.

Coupled to the need for protecting these species is the need to set aside reserve areas for them. All the endangered species and legal protection enacted by any country means nothing if it isn't enforced. It is not enough to legally defend a rare animal; it must also be physically protected. Broad tracts of fenced and patrolled nature reserve areas must be dedicated to this end.

Ideally, those last refuges of endangered species should be set aside for their protection, and wardens engaged to prevent poaching and tend to various tasks that ensure these species have adequate food, water, and care while they rebuild healthy breeding herds. While the animals are recovering from their man-made crisis, man must be educated to prevent a repetition of the crisis. And where education fails, severe penalties must be imposed on those who would seek to injure endangered animals.

When breeding herds are well developed, some of them should be reintroduced into the wild, away from protective fences and human tending. These species can then rejoin the balance of nature, fending for themselves as part of the broad scheme of Creation.

This process is the general theme proposed for any endangered species, anywhere in the world. But it is particularly important for the wildlife of the Middle East, where the destruction has been so extreme and so sudden.

All species, of course, have a natural right to existence. But the species of Scripture have a special right; they exist not in themselves alone, nor as just another animal inhabiting this planet. They are a living link to the origins of modern man. They exist as credible evidence for Scripture. They serve to enlighten our understanding of our most profound thinking and beliefs. Future generations will never truly understand the beauties, fears, inspiration, and stability seen by the writers of Scripture unless they too can gaze on the magnificence of a griffon in flight, or *bint al-raml* ("daughter of the sand"—the gazelle) lightly bounding across broad tracts of desert. These animals are Scripture incarnate.

If the work of the Holy Land Conservation Fund as described in *The Paper Ark* moves you to participate in the effort to restore the animals of Scripture to their ancestral home in the Holy Land, you are invited to contact Fund headquarters, 150 East 58th Street, New York, N.Y. 10022 (contributions to the Holy Land Fund are tax-deductible).

THE PAPER ARK

APES

"Be ye apes despised" (SURAH 7 : AL A'RAF : 166)

I T M A Y S E E M odd that the monkey, man's closest biological relative, is treated with relative indifference in Judaic and Islamic Scripture, and is completely ignored by the Christian testament.

Surely, monkeys were known to all three religions, and surely monkeys have many characteristics that would have made wonderful symbolic statements. Yet, for some reason, these intelligent primates are generally neglected.

Although theories of evolution were unheard of in the days of Scripture, the close physical similarity between man and monkey, and the monkey's undisputed superior intelligence compared to other animals, must have brought at least some people to wonder about this amusing primate. But such speculations could lead to dangerous questioning of a fundamentalist faith which assured categorically that God created man in His image. Obviously then, the monkey played his role not unlike any other animal.

Although it is of only little scriptural importance, it is interesting to note the great divergence in attitude Judaic and Islamic Scriptures hold toward the monkey. To the Jews, the monkey represented part of a great treasure and helped symbolize a thriving international commerce. For Moslems, the manlike creature was an animal of contempt.

The Islamic contempt for the monkey is found in the Koran. The anger of Allah descending on the unbeliever is found in the koranic description of: "Whom Allah has cursed him on whom His wrath hath fallen! Worse is he whose sort Allah hath turned some to apes and swine, and who serveth idols" (Surah 5: Al Ma'idah:60).

Warning the Moslem who would dare forsake his faith

after having accepted the message of Al Islam, the Koran says: "So when they took pride in that which they had been forbidden, We said unto them: Be ye apes despised and loathed" (Surah 7: Al'raf:166).

Conversely, Hebraic Scripture places the monkey among the jewels of the treasures imported by King Solomon thirty centuries ago: "For the king's ship went to Tarshish with the servants of Huram: every three years once came the ships of Tarshish bringing gold, and silver, ivory, and apes, and peacocks" (II Chronicles 9:21).

Although both the Bible and Koran are translated to read "apes," it is unlikely they mean the true anthropoid apes, such as the gorilla, for these are only found in the most remote areas, they're extremely difficult to capture, and until recently, they rarely survived very long in captivity. More likely, both Scriptures probably meant more common monkeys, which have been pets in tropical areas for centuries.

The description of Solomon's treasure gives us a fascinating insight into the extent of the king's trade during those very ancient days when humans were first starting to explore concepts of international commerce. Silver and gold, mentioned in the scriptural passage, could be found at several locales through the Mediterranean and Middle East. But ivory, monkeys, and peacocks meant long trade routes and contact with distant civilizations.

Although the scriptural passage from Chronicles says that Solomon's ships "went to Tarshish with the servants of Huram," a study of the sources of cargo can lead us to speculate that this trade could have extended much farther. First, Tarshish was a Phoenician colony in Spain, the gateway to the Atlantic, and Huram was the king of the Phoenician city of Tyre during the reign of Solomon. Thus, the passage would suggest that Solomon and Huram enjoyed a peaceful relationship and even beneficial trade arrangements. Some monkeys might have come from as far as the Atlantic coast of equatorial Africa, where the intrepid Phoenician sailors are reputed to have visited.

Another speculation could suggest that the monkeys might have even come from America. And there is some evidence that this might have been accomplished.

Thor Heyerdahl's Ra expedition proved that even an Egyptian papyrus raft, which was designed essentially for river traffic on the Nile, could have crossed the Atlantic. The Phoenicians, however, were greater traders, better navigators, and superior ship builders. If Egyptians could have made the journey, there is every reason to believe that the Phoenicians would have been even more capable of the trip.

Also, high on a Mexican mountain called Monte Alban, outside the city of Oaxaca, there is a very interesting bas-relief sculpture. Carved long before Columbus, the sculpture shows the profile of a man with a beard and dressed in Phoenician attire. The important matter to remember here is that the Indians living in America never grew beards. Beards were as impossible for them to grow as growing hair on the palms of one's hands would be for any other man. A sculpture of a man with a beard is more than coincidence. It means the pre-Columbian Indians of Mexico at one time had contact with men from the Old World. What appears to be Phoenician

clothing on the man in the sculpture further suggests that they had contact with Solomon's neighbors, if not with the merchants representing Solomon himself.

Indian traditions in the area also tell of stories of visitors from the East, from across the Atlantic. Indeed, when Cortez landed in Mexico, he found his conquest relatively easy because the Indians living there believe he was Quetzalcoatl, the powerful friend who had once visited them so many centuries before, and promised to return to deliver a new era of ascendancy.

Could the Quetzalcoatl have been a Phoenician merchant? Or even one of Solomon's merchants who were authorized to share in Phoenician trade? Could the monkeys that came back to Israel by way of Tarshish have originally come from America? Granted, these are speculations, but it is possible and only waits for some archaeologist to either prove or disprove.

But what grander jewel could have been for the mighty Solomon than importing a manlike primate from the far side of the earth?

Trade also expanded in the opposite direction. We know Solomon "made a navy of ships in Ezion-geber, which is beside Eloth, on the shore of the Red sea, in the land of Edom" (I Kings 9:26), and commissioned Hiram as the fleet's commander. Here, the seas open east, making possible trade along the Arabian coast, East Africa, and perhaps even India.

The possibility of trade with India is strengthened by the record that Hiram's fleet "came to Ophir" (I Kings 9:28). Ophir, some scholars believe, was a community along India's Malabar coast. For sure, monkeys were available there, and so was the *togei*, the Malabar name for the peacock. This bears a remarkable resemblance to the Hebrew name for the same bird, *tukki*.

Incidentally, it is said that one of Columbus' sailors was Jewish, and when they landed in America, this sailor saw a strange bird with beautiful colors. He remembered such a bird from reading Scripture and immediately named it *tukki*. If today's American Indians have a legitimate complaint that they still carry the burden of being misnamed by a confused explorer back in 1492, so does the bird that graces our feasting table every Thanksgiving.

ASSES (DOMESTIC)

"Behold, thy King cometh unto thee, meek, and sitting upon an ass" (MATTHEW 21:5)

WHEN JESUS PREPARED to enter Jerusalem on Palm Sunday, marking the most triumphant phase of his ministry, he chose to ride a humble ass.

Waiting on the Mount of Olives, just east of the city, Christ turned to two of his disciples, "Saying unto them, Go into the village over against you, and straightway ye shall find an ass tied, and a colt with her: loose them and bring them unto me. And if any man say ought unto you, ye shall say, The Lord hath need of them; and straightway he will send them. All this was done, that it might be fulfilled which was spoken by the prophet, saying, Tell ye the daughter of Sion, Behold, thy King cometh unto thee, meek, and sitting upon an ass, and a colt the foal of an ass" (Matthew 21:2–5).

The symbolism of this event had a profound affect on Christian theology, and, without the ass, such symbolism would have been substantially weakened. First, riding the modest animal fulfilled a prophesy: "O daughter of Jerusalem: behold, thy King cometh unto thee: he is just, and having salvation; lowly, and riding upon an ass, and upon a colt the foal of an ass" (Zechariah 9:9). But the episode had an even deeper meaning. Riding the ass, the symbol of humble servitude, Christ set an image that has survived in Christian philosophy to this day—the demonstrated disdain for temporal extravagance.

However, this event of Scripture was by no means the first time the ass was cast as the image of a humble servant. Domesticated in the Middle East centuries before Christ, the ass served as a riding and pack animal as well as for agricultural purposes. The Bible records that Israelites used the ass as far back as the patriarch Abraham (Genesis 24:35).

Even today, it is a common beast of burden in both the narrow streets of Middle Eastern cities and among the desert Bedouin.

The image of the ass was irrevocably cast at the time when the land of Israel was apportioned between the twelve wandering tribes. The tribe of Issachar, assigned the fertile agricultural lands southwest of the Sea of Galilee, was likened to "a strong ass couching down between two burdens: And he saw that rest was good, and the land that it was pleasant; and bowed his shoulder to bear, and became a servant unto tribute" (Genesis 49:14–15).

This submissive ass also figured into opening the land of Canaan to the Israelites on their return from the Egyptian bondage. Ignoring a commandment of God, Balaam, a Moabite aristocrat, was persuaded to join forces organized to repulse the coming Israelites. An angry God dispatched an angel to thwart Balaam's defiance. Appearing only to the ass that Balaam was riding, the angel caused the animal to behave erratically and with each abnormal action, Balaam beat the animal.

After a series of incidents and beatings, the ass finally collapsed. While the animal was on the ground at the feet of an infuriated Balaam, "the Lord opened the mouth of the ass, and said unto Balaam, What have I done unto thee, that thou has smitten me these three times? And Balaam said unto the ass, Because thou hast mocked me: I would there were a sword in mine hand, for now would I kill thee. And the ass said unto Balaam, Am not I thine ass, upon which thou has ridden ever since I was thine unto this day? was I ever wont to do so unto

thee? And he said, Nay" (Numbers 22:28–30).

At this point, the Bible adds, the angel appeared also to Balaam and made him realize his defiance of God. Balaam repented and subsequently obeyed divine command, receiving the Israelites warmly.

That angel also delivered one of the earliest prohibitions against cruelty to animals, as well as enjoining Balaam to be thankful for the reactions of his animal: "And the ass saw me, and turned from me these three times: unless she had turned from me, surely now also I had slain thee, and saved her alive" (Numbers 22:33).

Mosaic law laid down some of the elemental rules concerning treatment of animals, and the ass in particular. Even the beast of an enemy deserved compassion: "If thou meet thine enemy's ox or his ass going astray, thou shalt surely bring it back to him again. If thou see the ass of him that hateth thee lying under his burden, and wouldest forbear to help him, thou shalt help with him" (Exodus 23:4–5)

Another Mosaic law, "Thou shalt not plow with an ox and an ass together" (Deuteronomy 22:10), suggests the stronger ox would place an undue burden on the ass by causing it to work with equal strength.

This tradition of sympathy for a beast of burden is brought into the New Testament. Christ, defending the need for works of compassion on the Sabbath, questioned his tormentors: "Which of you shall have an ass or an ox fallen into a pit, and will not straightway pull him out on the sabbath day?" (Luke 14:5), thus broadening the toleration of the formerly strict prohibition of any labor on the Sabbath.

Perhaps because of its submissiveness, the ass is often characterized as a stupid animal to be scorned and maligned. Koranic literature has an almost comic simile concerning this image of the ass: "The likeness of those who are entrusted with the Law of Moses, yet apply it not, is the likeness of the ass carrying books" (Surah 62: Al Jum'ah:5).

A bit more gruesome is God's commandment of a scornful burial for Jehoiakim, son of King Josiah: "He shall be buried with the burial of an ass, drawn and cast forth beyond the gates of Jerusalem" (Jeremiah 22:19).

The domestic ass (*Equus asinus domesticus*) is the descendant of various breeds of wild ass which are often identified according to their places of origin—Nubian, Persian, Somali, etc. While the common ass is frequently the object of derision, the Damascus variety is usually held in esteem. Surefooted and pure white in color, the Damascus ass is the elite of its species. And so it has been since biblical times: "Bless ye the Lord. Speak, ye that ride on white asses, ye that sit in judgment" (Judges 5:9–10).

BEARS

"We roar all like bears" (ISAIAH 59:11)

THERE are few crimes in this world more barbaric and reprehensible than the mass slaughter of children. And when such a deed of infamy occurs in Scripture, it is the bear that is assigned to be the executioner.

The story occurs at the time when the kingdoms of Israel and Judah were divided. The prophet Elisha, journeying to Mount Carmel, passed through the village of Beth-el, the enchanting community where the patriarch Abraham once talked with God, and where Jacob dreamed his divine vision of a Jewish legacy.

Along the road, Elisha was tormented by a multitude of children. "Go up, thou bald head; go up, thou bald head," they mocked the prophet. "And he turned back, and looked on them," the Bible records, "and cursed them in the name of the Lord. And there came forth two she bears out of the wood, and tare forty and two children of them" (II Kings 2:23, 24).

Those who would scorn a prophet are condemned to a harsh punishment. This punishment is truly an act of vengeance in which the disciplined experience the terror and pain of retribution. Unlike the striking of a bolt of lightning, or the swift rush of a lion, the bear's attack is slow, ponderous, and mauling. This ambling heavyweight has come to symbolize unmerciful brute force.

The ancient Hebrews called the bear *dov*, a name that stems from the onomatopoeic verb *dovav*—"to move at a slow pace." With this identity, the bear lumbers through Scripture wielding a harsh and crushing power.

David's strength and prowess were exhibited at an early age when, as a simple shepherd boy, he killed bears that had attacked his flocks (I Samuel 17:36).

But the slayer of bears eventually developed a bearlike temperament himself, and Hushai warned David's son, Absalom: "thou knowest thy father and his men, that they be mighty men, and they be chafed in their minds, as a bear robbed of her whelps in the field: and thy father is a man of war" (II Samuel 17:8).

If a bear is typically seen as colossal and terrifying, then this image is intensified when a she-bear is fighting for her cubs. This is the time when the bear becomes most enraged and is willing to risk any odds to protect her youngsters.

This characteristic is seen again in a metaphor where the prophet Hosea records the word of God planning the destruction of idolators: "I will meet them as a bear that is bereaved of her whelps, and will rend the caul of their heart" (Hosea 13:8).

Solomon also recognized the anger of a she-bear deprived of her cubs, and wrote in his Proverbs: "Let a bear robbed of her whelps meet a man, rather than a fool in his folly" (Proverbs 17:12). Here, the great King suggests that even the mighty bear may assume the role of an injured party, and furthermore, it is better for the wrongdoer to face justice as a person of courage and self-esteem rather than to cower in deceit and stupidity.

The mighty King also perceived a few "bears" in his own profession and warned that a wicked ruler is like "a ranging bear" (Proverbs 28:15).

The bear that appears in Scripture is most probably the Syrian bear (*Ursus arctus syriacus*), a light brown cousin of the common European brown bear. Driven from its traditional habitat, this variety today is rare and may only be seen in zoos. There currently are plans, however, to reintroduce some of these powerful giants into remote and protected areas of biblical lands, particularly around the north of Israel.

One reserve area planned at Hai Bar North seems particularly well suited for the mighty Syrian bear. The reserve is located in the northern Galilee, where the Hai Bar society is designing a predator complex. Here, the great bear can be reintroduced into a secure portion of its ancestral habitat without posing any threat to neighboring kibbutzim.

While scriptural references about the bear are generally accurate, later legends have distorted our general perception of the animal. Bears are generally cautious of humans, and almost never attack without provocation. The greatest provocation, as we see in Scripture, is taking cubs from a mother bear. This truly enrages her.

Bears are known to be very individualistic, each one with a different and unpredictable personality. And the image of a bear standing on its hind legs and swinging its massive claws in an attack is totally false. Bears are very unbalanced when standing on two feet, and have great difficulty walking this way, much less attacking. When they do attack, it is invariably with all four feet on the ground. Claws rarely figure as important weapons to a bear—it does most of its fighting with its teeth. Claws are usually reserved for tearing into honeycombs and other foods.

Bears are plantigrade animals, which means they walk on the entire sole of their feet, much like a man. They are not known for having very good hearing or sight, but they have a

tremendous sense of smell, as many woodsmen who have lost a sizzling breakfast know.

Bears, incidentally, do not squeeze their opponents into submission. The bear hug is an invention of human wrestlers.

Because bears are bulky and awkward, they are not well equipped for hunting, as, say, a large cat is. The bear must use strategies in stalking, and one of these strategies is the ambush. Jeremiah knew of this, and used the image as he decried his spiritual distress. Fatalistically, Jeremiah saw his destiny lying before him "as a bear lying in wait" (Lamentations 3:10).

Bears figure significantly in the final judgment and Messianic prophesy. In describing the peaceable kingdom of the Messiah, Isaiah notes, "And the cow and the bear shall feed; their young ones shall lie down together" (Isaiah 11:7).

But the prophet realized the peaceable kingdom was still a long way off, and that humanity, in general, was in pretty bad shape. Perhaps he, too, had the vision of the she-bear robbed of her cubs when he wrote, "We roar all like bears, . . . we look for judgment, but there is none; for salvation, but it is far off from us" (Isaiah 59:11).

But that judgment will come, and it will be harsh. One prophesy anticipates that it is foolish to "desire the day of the Lord," claiming it will bring a terrible dilemma. Bringing the mighty bear to the height of authority, the prophet Amos promises those who run from a corrupt world to meet eternal judgment will be confounded: "As if a man did flee from a lion, and a bear met him" (Amos 5:19).

BEES

". . . and chased you, as bees do" (DEUTERONOMY 1:44)

THEN GOD led Moses to the threshold of a "land flowing with milk and honey" (Exodus 13:5). And any land flowing with honey is sure to be swarming with bees.

The bee was a common insect in ancient Israel. Mention of the bee's honey in Scripture is usually a symbol of great sweetness and joy. But mention of the bee itself usually focuses on its sharp stinger, with appropriate reference to episodes of turbulence and affliction. The bee's honey is a sweet nectar, but its sting is a painful thorn.

The sweetness of the bee's honey reaches several symbolic levels in Scripture. The human sensuality of the Canticles develops a soothing image: "Thy lips, O my spouse, drop as the honeycomb: honey and milk are under thy tongue" (Song of Songs 4:11).

In Proverbs the symbolism is drawn to an intellectual level, with the sweetness of honey likened to the sweetness of wisdom: "My son, eat thou honey, because it is good; and the honeycomb, which is sweet to thy taste: So shall the knowledge of wisdom be unto thy soul: when thou has found it, then there shall be a reward, and thy expectation shall not be cut off" (Proverbs 24:13–14).

The affinity established between honey and wisdom continues into Isaiah's Messianic prophesy: "Butter and honey shall he [the Messiah] eat, that he may know how to refuse the evil, and choose the good" (Isaiah 7:15).

Bees enter the prophesy three verses later, with the description of divine judgment against the oppressors of Israel: "And it shall come to pass in that day, that the Lord shall hiss . . . for the bee that is in the land of Assyria" (Isaiah 7:18).

The Assyrians were not the only tormentors of Israel to be

likened to the unrelenting bees. Moses reminded the tribes of a time that they went to war, even though God commanded them to remain at peace: "And the Amorites, which dwelt in that mountain, came out against you, and chased you, as bees do, and destroyed you in Seir, even unto Hormah" (Deuteronomy 1:44).

But vengeance against those enemy nations that had stung Israel was also pledged: "They compassed me about like bees; they are quenched as the fire of thorns: for in the name of the Lord I will destroy them" (Psalms 118:12).

While farmers in the ancient lands of the Bible undoubtedly kept honeybees, it was also common for people to seek, and eat, wild honey. King Saul's army encountered wild honey as they chased the Philistines through the Judean hills (I Samuel 14:26). And John the Baptist lived on a diet of "locusts and wild honey" (Matthew 3:4).

A whole book of the Koran is named for the bee, "An-Nahl." Working through extended metaphors concerning bees, and other animals of nature, An-Nahl develops the theme that social inequality is part of the grand scheme of Allah for an ordered universe.

Using the bee as an illustration, An-Nahl says: "And thy Lord inspired the bee, saying: Choose thou habitations in the hills and in the trees and in that which they thatch; Then eat of all fruits, and follow the ways of thy Lord, made smooth. There cometh forth from their bellies a drink of diverse hues, wherein is healing for mankind. Lo! herein is indeed a portent for people who reflect" (Surah 16: An-Nahl: 68, 69).

The Islamic image of the bee is found in its sense of community and social order, with queens, drones, and workers each performing their predetermined task. The result of ordered work, with its chosen habitat and diet, is "a drink of diverse hues"—the bee's honey, the sweetness of life.

On a broader plane, the bee metaphor in An-Nahl may be interpreted as divinely inspired community life being the means to the succulent reward, a "healing for mankind."

BEHEMOTHS

"Behold now behemoth" (JOB 40:15)

IRONICALLY, the identity of this great creature, called "the chief of the ways of God," is shrouded in mystery. Althought it is mentioned only once in Scripture, the giant behemoth has wandered far. It is a familiar image that has ranged into dozens of languages and scores of legends and stories around the world. But the single source reference, in the Book of Job, includes a detailed, ten-verse description; plenty to start a speculative inquiry.

Behold now behemoth, which I made with thee; he eateth grass as an ox.

Lo now, his strength is in his loins, and his force is in the navel of his belly.

He moveth his tail like a cedar: the sinews of his stones are wrapped together.

His bones are as strong pieces of brass; his bones are like bars of iron.

He is the chief of the ways of God: he that made him can make his sword to approach unto him.

Surely the mountains bring him forth food, where all the beasts of the field play.

He lieth under the shady trees, in the covert of the reed, and fens.

The shady trees cover him with their shadow; the willows of the brook compass him about.

Behold, he drinketh up a river, and hasteth not: he trusteth that he can draw up Jordan into his mouth.

He taketh it with his eyes: his nose pierceth through snares. (Job 40:15–24)

The meaning of these verses fits well with the other animal-oriented portions of the Book of Job. Simply, God is

impressing Job, and all humanity, with His creative powers. At the same time, humanity is forced to recognize its own meager abilities. The whole description of the behemoth points to the ultimate of physical strength, yet, in a critical passage, God says that He "can make his sword to approach unto him." Even the mightiest beast of Creation is powerless before the might of God.

While the symbolic value of the behemoth is quite clear—the inability of anything in Creation to challenge the power of the Creator—we still can't be sure precisely what animal Job had in mind when he described this great creature. But with Job's description, and some help from various sciences, scholars have narrowed an investigation down to four possibilities: the hippopotamus, the water buffalo, the elephant, and a purely mythical creature.

To begin our inquiry, we may eliminate the theory that the behemoth is a creature of myth. Surely, any zoologist would claim that there is insufficient information in the Book of Job to identify the behemoth as any known animal, but the evidence that the behemoth is a real animal, regardless of its identity, is too overwhelming. Although many respected scholars have argued that the behemoth is myth, their arguments just don't make sense.

First, the whole point of the behemoth story is to illustrate the impotence of the natural world before the power of a supernatural God; Creation is weaker than the Creator. For Job to invent a mythical behemoth would destroy the whole meaning of the episode, for myth is the antithesis of reality. In myth there is no rule to say who is stronger.

Also, Job was an acute observer of nature, and perhaps one of the most accurate naturalists of the ancient world. He wrote with both sensitivity and understanding of the wonders of the natural world. He made precise observations of vipers, lions, ostrich, and many other species that inhabited his homeland, and each of these observations served to depict the magnificence of God's Creation. It would be far out of context for Job, such a reliable naturalist, to invent a species when he was familiar enough with real creatures to make his point.

Furthermore, the behemoth is described as "the chief of the ways of God," with "chief" also translatable as "foremost" or "first." Would it not be highly illogical to suggest that the foremost beast of Creation is not truly a part of the natural world, but only a product of a man's imagination?

So what is this behemoth? According to Job's description, the animal is certainly herbivorous, and probably bovine. It is a strong-boned animal with tremendous gut strength—a real brute. The behemoth has a tail that sways like a cedar tree, it has a prodigious appetite, it is found both in the mountains and in swamps and rivers, and likes to loll in the shade. It also has an amazing capacity for drinking, and has a rather peculiar nose.

The hippopotamus, water buffalo, and elephant all have reasonably good cases for claiming to be the behemoth. And with recent archaeological discoveries in the Middle East, there's no reason to suspect that the inquiry will forever be limited to these three possibilities. It should not be a great surprise if tomorrow someone unearths the bones of some long-extinct animal near the course of the Jordan River, assembles a skeleton, and claims, "Behold now behemoth."

The hippopotamus has a strong claim to the title "behemoth." For certain, it fits much of Job's description. The hippo is an animal of enormous size and strength, and it has an appetite to match its size. It is a plant eater, inhabits watery locales, and has a mouth that could open against the Jordan better than any other contender. Furthermore, in modern Hebrew, the word for hippopotamus is *behemoth*. Most scholars tend to agree that the hippopotamus is the behemoth of Scripture, but being in agreement doesn't necessarily mean being correct.

The argument for the hippopotamus is both strengthened and weakened by the study of etymology, the history of word derivation. Just because modern Israelis call their hippopotamus *behemoth* does not mean their ancestors did.

In the land of the pharaohs, where the Hebrew tribes were held as captive slaves, the word for hippopotamus is *p-ehe-mau* —a word with a striking similiarity to "behemoth." But there are some problems with this similiarity.

Just as our own "hippopotamus" may be traced back to the ancient Greek to mean "river horse" (*hippos*, "horse"; *potamus*, "river"), the *p-ehe-mau* comes from an ancient Egyptian tongue and means "river ox." But here we have a name that might more properly be given to the water buffalo, a true ox. Could it be that "behemoth" and "p-ehe-mau" describe the same animal, and that animal originally was a river ox, a water buffalo, and only in later centuries did the name fall on the broad shoulders of the hippopotamus?

The water buffalo's claim to the title "behemoth" is enhanced by a curious matter of Jewish law. Wild animals (*hayyah*) and domestic animals (*behemah*) are separated into two groups by the Jewish talmudic code. Over the centuries, a confusion developed concerning a few species that at one time might have domesticated, but subsequently reverted back to the wild. The main argument centered on the wild ox, an animal that scholars suspected was once domesticated. And this argument can also be extended to the water buffalo.

The name "behemoth" is closely related to the talmudic *behemah*, and this may suggest that the behemoth had once been a domestic animal, or at least is closely related to domestic animals—even though Job's behemoth is obviously wild. Water buffalo have been domesticated in many parts of the world. Hippopotamuses have not.

Now, when Job makes his initial description of the behemoth, saying "he eateth grass as an ox," there may be a meaning that is much deeper than simply claiming the animal is herbivorous. One of the tests as to whether an animal is accepted as "kosher" in Jewish dietary law rests in its ability to ruminate, or "chew the cud." The water buffalo, just as the ox, has this ability.

There are several other characteristics of the water buffalo that suggest this animal is the real behemoth. It fits most of Job's description, being a large and powerful animal with obvious muscle fiber in its sinuous physique. It has strong bones, has been found on mountain sides and swamps, lingers in the shade, and has a healthy drinking ability.

But many of these observations can also be made of the elephant. It is the largest of land animals, and certainly fits the general image of a behemoth. Its colossal size, herbivorous diet, stout bones, and inclination to tarry in the shade surely fit many of the requirements. And its sweeping tail certainly bears an extraordinary resemblance to a cedar tree swaying in the breeze.

But the elephant's trunk is its best claim for being the behemoth. Dropping his long and flexible proboscis into a water course, the elephant can draw up a tremendous quantity of fluid. And because of the elephant's unique anatomy, with the trunk apparently flowing from the forehead, it may truly seem that he draws water "with his eyes." Finally, Job's last verse also seems to point toward the elephant: "his nose pierceth through snares."

It is quite possible that the ancient Hebrews may have been familiar with all three of the likely possibilities for behemoth. The hippopotamus lived in Israel during the Pleistocene era—long before man was keeping records—but the Hebrew tribes might also have seen the species during their Egyptian captivity, since the hippopotamus lived along the Egyptian part of the Nile until the nineteenth century.

The elephant, also, is no stranger to the land of Israel. During the days of the Patriarchs, the Egyptian Pharaoh Thutmose III conquered the Middle East, and, records note, he was fond of hunting the great pachyderm in the lush valley of the Orontes River, which rises in the mountains of Lebanon. Elephant ivory was highly prized during the period of the Kingdom of Israel, and the Book of Maccabees records how the Seleucid Antiochus Epiphanes used elephant cavalry in his campaigns against the Jews.

But this writer believes the water buffalo is the behemoth of the Book of Job. The water buffalo inhabited Israel throughout biblical times, living in the northern swamps around Hulah in the Galilee. The growth of the human community in this area during recent centuries has chased the water buffalo out, but, quite by accident, Israeli troops encountered a small herd of them running wild during the 1967 campaign to take the Golan Heights. These water buffalo were brought back to the Hulah, where they have bred prolifically within the protection of a nature reserve. Here, at the headwaters of the Jordan, may well be the descendants of that animal which amazed Job and made him call it "the chief of the ways of God."

The hippopotamus, the elephant, and the water buffalo—each has a good claim to the title "behemoth." And no one knows who may make an equally credible case for the rhinoceros or some species of antelope, or even some extinct animal whose bones still lie deep in the earth of ancient Israel.

CAMELS

". . . regard the camels, how they are created" (SURAH 88: AL-GHASHIYA:17)

On AL-GHASHIYA, the Islamic Day of Judgment, the Koran says humanity will be divided into two camps, the saved and the damned. The damned will be cursed for eternity; but those who have followed the message of Al-Islam will be saved and will rest in a blissful serenity, reclining on silken carpets and contemplating the wonders of Creation. And among these wonders, they will "regard the camels."

Doubtlessly, the Arabian camel (*Camelus dromedarius*) is one of the masterpieces of Creation. No other creature can match its ability to survive and work in the most hostile of desert climates. And these unique abilities make the camel an important factor in the Scriptures of all three monotheistic religions born in the arid Middle East.

The camel attains its most significant religious symbolism in the Koran where it appears in a metaphor describing the

greatest gift of God. The episode is found in Al-A'raf (The Heights). Allah sends a she-camel to the tribe of Thamud as a divine gift and as a test of the tribe's fidelity. When the animal arrives, the prophet Salih exhorts the tribe: "Lo! this is the camel of Allah, a token unto you; so let her feed in Allah's earth, and touch her not with hurt lest painful torment seize you."

But the tribe ridiculed Salih, refused to recognize Allah, and took the camel, which they mistreated in their own use. Al-A'raf continues, recording that the tribe "hamstrung the she-camel, and they flouted the commandment of their Lord, they said: O Salih! Bring upon us that thou threatenest if thou art indeed of those sent."

The tribe soon found that Salih was a true prophet of Allah and the camel was a divine gift. "So the earthquake seized them, and morning found them prostrate in their dwelling places" (Surah 7: Al-A'raf:73–78).

In this episode, the camel is a symbol of divine benevolence for those who have faith in God, and divine wrath for those who refuse the gift of faith. In Islamic terms, the camel story is a metaphor for the gift of religion, Al-Islam (The Surrender), the greatest gift of all. Those who accept and use their gift wisely will prosper, and those who abuse the gift and spurn God are doomed.

A large and muscular animal, the camel is best known as a beast of burden that is capable of carrying hundreds of pounds across wide expanses of desert. Although some experts claim it was domesticated around 1200 B.C.E., biblical evidence suggests a date several centuries earlier. Camels are mentioned as part of the patriarch Abraham's wealth (Genesis 24:10).

Starting with the reference in Genesis, the camel became a symbol of material wealth. The Ishmeelites, prosperous merchants from Gilead who bought the young Joseph as a slave, traveled in a caravan "with their camels bearing spicery and balm and myrrh, going to carry it down to Egypt" (Genesis 37:25). Three thousand camels were counted as part of Job's wealth before his misfortunes, and six thousand camels were a measure of his wealth after he had survived his trials (Job 1:3, 42:12).

Perhaps the most spectacular array of camels found in Scripture was gathered by the Queen of Sheba in her attempt to impress the mighty King Solomon. "And she came to Jerusalem with a very great train, with camels that bare spices, and very much gold, and precious stones" (I Kings 10:2). The desert Queen's entourage must have been one of the most astonishing sights of the ancient world.

While ancient man counted the camel as a measure of wealth and an integral part of commerce, the "ship of the desert" was also considered useful as an instrument of war. By the time of Gideon, camel cavalry was a formidable weapon, and the Bible narrates a threatening advance of the Midianites: "their camels were without number, as the sand by the sea side for multitude" (Judges 7:12). It was only a shrewd ruse that repulsed the mounted invaders and saved Gideon and the Israelites.

The reason for the camel's superior value in both peace and war lies in its anatomy and metabolism. Its body is strong and well suited for carrying heavy loads. Broad feet keep it from sinking into soft sand, and a coarse, hairy coat insulates it from the burning sun. Long eyelashes and muscular nostrils protect its eyes, nose, and throat from dust and sand blown by desert storms.

But the camel's metabolism is its most unique asset. Long periods of food and water deprivation in intense heat demand particular adjustments if an animal is to survive. To save precious water, a camel can let its body temperature fluctuate, increasing in the heat of the day as much as ten degrees Fahrenheit, only to lose the heat by radiation into the cool of the evening.

Camels have a remarkable ability for surviving extreme losses of body water. On a long journey across a desert, a camel may lose more than 20 percent of its weight to dehydration without serious effect. If a man lost this percentage of water, he would most likely be dead.

While most mammals dehydrate through both blood and

tissue simultaneously, the camel loses tissue water only. Consequently, a camel that appears emaciated from dehydration may actually be in fine health, with his circulatory system functioning unimpaired. And after this type of dehydration, a camel can replace all his lost water simply by taking a long drink at the nearest well or oasis. Again, this type of replenishment could kill any other mammal by bloating and bursting vital red blood corpuscles.

A part of the Koran alludes to the camel's prodigious drinking capacity, and gives followers of Mohammed an insight into one of the tortures of Hell. "And thereon ye [the damned] will drink of boiling water, Drinking even as a camel drinketh" (Surah 56: Al-Waqi-ah:54–55).

Considering a thirsty camel can drink twenty-five gallons of water in ten minutes, the consumption of this much boiling water seems a most terrible torture for any sinner.

A final point on metabolism is the camel's hump. The hump is actually a large lump of fat which serves as a food store for long journeys. The fat is consolidated in one place, keeping the rest of the animal lean and cool. And a sharp-eyed camel trader can simply look at the hump to get an idea of how the camel has been treated. A firm, upright hump means it has been well fed with suitable food, and a flabby, drooping hump is a sign of malnutrition.

The camel is the largest desert animal, and its great stature has cast it as a scriptural symbol for enormity. In the New Testament the camel's great size becomes a symbol for matters of great importance. Jesus, criticizing the Scribes and Pharisees as being pedantic with minor matters, exclaimed: "Woe unto you, scribes and Pharisees, hypocrites! for ye pay tithe of mint and anise and cummin, and have omitted the weightier matters of the law, judgment, mercy, and faith: these ought ye to have done, and not to leave the other undone. Ye blind guides, which strain at a gnat, and swallow a camel" (Matthew 23:23–24).

Both the New Testament and the Koran have passages that the camel's size in metaphors describing the difficulty of entering Heaven: "And again I say unto you, It is easier for a camel to go through the eye of a needle, than for a rich man to enter into the kingdom of God" (Matthew 19:24).

"Lo! they who deny Our revelations and scorn them, for them the gates of Heaven will not open nor will they enter the Garden until the camel goeth through the needle's eye" (Surah 7: Al-A'raf:40).

The camel is forbidden as food in the Old Testament: "Nevertheless these shall ye not eat of them that chew the cud or of them that divide the hoof; as the camel, because he cheweth the cud, but divideth not the hoof; he is unclean unto you" (Leviticus 11:4).

Although the Koran and the New Testament do not forbid the eating of camel, neither suggests that camel meat is much of a delicacy. The Koran does mention, however, that when a camel dies, it may be used to "feed the beggar and supplicant" (Surah 22: Al-Majj:36).

Apparently, the camel's juices are as distasteful as his disposition. And his disposition is anything but savory. The Bedouin, nomadic desert tribesmen who are dependent on the camel to this day, have an adage that captures this concept: "There are no longer any wild camels in the desert; and no one claims to own a tame one either."

CATTLE

". . . and the cattle upon a thousand hills" (PSALMS 50:10)

CATTLE are a key to civilization. They fulfill vital roles that permit man to live in permanent communities.

Moses knew this, and it is no wonder that when he argued with Pharaoh for the release of the Hebrew tribes, he demanded: "Our cattle also shall go with us; there shall not an hoof be left behind" (Exodus 10:26). Pharaoh rejected the demand, and the Hebrews were fated for much more hardship, but in the end they did escape Egypt, and they took their cattle with them.

The Exodus was a difficult time for the escaping Hebrew tribes and tending cattle through this time made the journey an even greater hardship. Cattle require prodigious quantities of food and water, commodities that were extremely rare in much of the desert they had to cross. When they were confronted by armed Edomites, Moses pleaded with their King:

"We will go by the high way: and if I and my cattle drink of thy water, then I will pay for it" (Numbers 20:19). Again, Moses was refused, and he was forced to take a circuitous route back through more barren desert.

The hardship was well worth the effort, for the tribes eventually reached their Promised Land of Canaan, and their cattle repaid them many times over for the forty-year effort of the journey. Domestic cattle (*Bos taurus domesticus*) gave these wandering tribes a vital foundation for the land that was to become the Kingdom of Israel—agriculture. This is illustrated in the proverb: "Where no oxen are, the crib is clean: but much increase is by the strength of the ox" (Proverbs 14:4). Without the powerful ox, that castrated male bovine, the rocky soil of Canaan could not profitably be turned; without agriculture, "the crib is clean," no food could be stored, and the Hebrew tribes would have been forced to continue their nomadic wanderings.

These ancient Hebrews knew their cattle as *baqar*, stemming from a verb meaning "to plough." The Arabic name for the same beast, *baqarah*, stems from the same root.

Cattle also provided many other necessities—meat, milk, and leather—but it was their strength under the farmer's yoke that let the tribes settle with a fixed food supply. And this settlement enabled them to build a nation with the great cities of Jerusalem, Beersheva, Hebron, and Megiddo.

Cattle were essential tools in the building of the Israelite community, but like all valued tools, there was a tendency toward overuse. Because of this, Jewish law includes some of man's first animal protection legislation. Dietary laws considered cattle as clean meat, but as a humane gesture, they prohibit stewing the flesh of a calf in its mother's milk. Furthermore, the slaughtering of a cow and its calf on the same day was also considered odious: "And whether it be cow or ewe, ye shall not kill it and her young both in one day" (Leviticus 22:28). The hardworking beast was permitted a day of rest: "and on the seventh day thou shalt rest: that thine ox and thine ass may rest" (Exodus 23:12). It was also permitted to taste the fruits of its labor: "Thou shall not muzzle the ox when he treadeth out the corn" (Deuteronomy 25:4).

Compassion was ordered when a beast was in danger: "Thou shalt not see thy brother's ass or his ox fall down by the way, and hide thyself from them: thou shalt surely help him to lift them up again" (Deuteronomy 22:4).

Several verses of the Bible relate exacting rules for the sacrifice of cattle as an offering to God. Such sacrifices are also mentioned in the Koran, for Islam looks to the ancient Hebrews as the progenitors of their faith. In the koranic chapter Al-Baqarah (The Cow), Mohammed tells of Moses' requirements for a sacrificial cow: "Lo! He saith, Verily she is a cow neither with calf nor immature: [she is] between the two conditions. . . . Verily she is a yellow cow. Bright is her colour, gladdening beholders. . . . Verily, she is a cow unyoked; she plougheth not the soil nor watereth the tilth; whole and without mark" (Surah 2: Al-Baqarah:68–71).

The Koran also recognizes the value of the bovine beast: "And of the cattle [Allah created] some for burdens, some for food. Eat of that which Allah hath bestowed upon you, and follow not the footsteps of the devil, for lo! he is an open foe to you" (Surah 6: Al-An'am:143).

Cattle were such important animals to both the Hebrews and Arabs that sometimes wayward members of these peoples began to worship them. With the absence of Moses, the Hebrews made a golden calf as an idol of worship. The enraged patriarch returned to his people: "And he took the calf which they had made, and burnt it in the fire, and ground it to powder, and strawed it upon the water, and made the children of Israel drink of it" (Exodus 32:20).

The Koran relates the story of four tribes that set their cattle free and began to worship them: "Allah hath not appointed anything in the nature of Bahirah or a Sa'ibah or a Wasilah or a Hami, but those who disbelieve invent a lie against Allah" (Surah 5: Al Ma'idah:103).

. Perhaps it was this proclivity toward reverting to carnal

paganism that inspired the prophet to condemn the hypocrites: "For Israel slideth back as a back-sliding heifer" (Hosea 4:16).

However, these relapses are an exception rather than the rule, and for Jews and Moslems cattle maintained a position of necessity and repute.

Cattle are almost unmentioned in Christian Scripture, and most probably this is because Christians, unlike Jews and Moslems, were not interested in establishing a theocratic state. Christian thought looks to the spiritual state and shows little concern for building earthly communities. Thus, there is little concern for the necessities of human cities and the beasts of burden and food that make these cities possible.

The Middle East is not naturally suited for large-scale cattle farming. Limited precipitation in winter, followed by an extremely long dry season with soaring temperatures, reduces the periods of rich grass growth to between one and three months. The steep hillsides are not readily adaptable to awkward cattle. Drinking water is not abundant.

However, technical advances in agriculture have provided hybrids that do well in irrigated soil. Advances in scientific animal husbandry have produced new breeds of cattle which survive the intense summer heat much better than any of their temperate zone relatives. Successes in modern agriculture have been so great that cattle today are kept profitably in one of the most parched areas of the world, more than twelve hundred feet below sea level along the shores of the Dead Sea.

CONIES

". . . and the rocks for the conies" (PSALMS 104:18)

AMBLING THROUGH the wadis, those dried-out riverbeds of the Middle East, is a humble creature called the coney.

It is a small mammal, a timid and pudgy creature that looks something like a groundhog. But Scripture has bestowed a great honor on this modest little creature, for in the Book of Proverbs, the coney (*Hyrax syriacus*) is observed to possess the virtue of wisdom.

Proverbs, one of the seats of biblical wisdom, recognized the diminutive coneys "are little upon the earth," but quickly added "they are exceeding wise" (Proverbs 30:24).

Many observers, on first watching the coney, might remark that they seem a bit clumsy and dull-witted. The Bible concedes this, but still finds wisdom: "The conies are but a feeble folk, yet make they their houses in the rocks" (Proverbs 30:26).

This leaves us with two questions: How does the Bible interpret the concept of wisdom, and what has it to do with living among rocks?

Of the various comments concerning wisdom made by King Solomon, there is one that is particularly well suited for this situation: "When wisdom entereth into thine heart," the monarch said, "discretion shall preserve thee" (Proverbs 2:10, 11). One view of wisdom, then, is the ability to be wary in matters of personal safety. There is also a spiritual interpretation to this passage, which may also mean that through wisdom, a person may prudently choose the proper path to salvation. In short, it is wisdom that guides man along the paths established by God.

Now, back to the coney. The Proverbial observations of

the coney serve as a metaphor for the discretion of spiritual wisdom. As wisdom is the guide to the coney's physical safety among the rocks of the wadi, so wisdom also is man's guide to spiritual safety.

And the coney does flourish among the rocks. Its legs, tail, and ears all appear short for its body, giving it the ability to slip through the narrowest of passages in the jumble of loose rocks that clutter the arid watercourses. Hard, hooflike nails on its feets are well suited for digging into the gravel at the wadi's floor. Its whole anatomy seems to be perfectly designed for finding shelter among the rocks, and these rocks form an almost impenetrable barrier for the predatory jackals, cats, and griffon vultures that would otherwise count the coney among their foremost delicacies.

Indeed, even the Hebrew name by which Solomon knew this animal, *shafan*, alludes to its cautious character. It means "hider."

Although the coney is not considered a truly gregarious animal, it does live in a loose social grouping that affords some additional protection. When most of a colony of coneys are out foraging for food in a wadi, they have sentinels posted at suitable observation posts. If a predator is seen, the sentinel cries with a shrill bark, warning of the approach of danger and sending the entire colony scurrying for "their houses in the rocks."

The Bible labels the coney as an unclean animal: "And the coney, because he cheweth the cud, but divideth not the hoof; he is unclean unto you" (Leviticus 11:5). Repeated in Deuteronomy 14:7, this observation is not exactly accurate. Although the coney appears to chew the cud, this is only a nervous habit, not unlike the rabbit twitching its nose. The coney does not have the digestive capabilities of a ruminant animal.

While the coney is found through many areas of the Middle East, Scripture gives us one verse that helps us to pinpoint at least one of its ancestoral lairs: "The high hills are a refuge for the wild goats; and the rocks for the conies" (Psalms 104:18). This location is most probably in the ravine Nahal David, a wadi near the oasis of En Gedi on the western edge of the Dead Sea. Here the psalmist David spent part of his exile and himself hid among the rocks to avoid the predacious spies and soldiers of King Saul.

David followed the wisdom of the coney and survived to become one of the greatest Kings of Israel. The goats, or more properly Nubian ibex, a kind of wild mountain goat, still inhabit the wadi. And, of course, so do the conies. They've been there at least three thousand years, and most likely the ones that live there today are the direct descendants of those seen by David, and given the honor of being included in Scripture as the image of wisdom.

DEER (FALLOW)

". . . a young hart upon the mountains of spices" (SONG OF SONGS 8:14)

THE FALLOW DEER is a gentle creature, the image of grace and speed.

Called *ayyal* in the ancient Hebrew of the Bible, which probably includes the two species of fallow deer once found in Israel, these species are translated into English Bibles as "hind" for the female and "hart" for the male.

The two species—the common fallow deer (*Dama dama*) and the Mesopotamian fallow deer (*Dama mesopotamica*)—both lived in the cool forests of northern Israel, Lebanon, and Syria. But centuries of unrestricted timber cutting destroyed most of this natural habitat and forced the fallow deer to leave. Scripture does, however, give us a clue concerning the fallow deer, their habitat, and the striking beauty that people saw in these gentle creatures thousands of years ago.

The fallow deer is identified with the tribe of Naphtali, the people who lived in the fertile hills of northern Galilee. Here, with the mountains of Golan rising to the east and Lebanon towering to the west, Naphtali lived in one of the most remote and idyllic areas of ancient Israel: "Nephtali is a hind let loose: he giveth goodly words" (Genesis 49:21).

When Moses blessed the Hebrew tribes before they entered the Promised Land, he addressed these people of the deer: "And of Naphtali he said, O Naphtali, satisfied with favour, and full with the blessing of the Lord" (Deuteronomy 33:23). This blessing seems to apply to the fallow deer as much as to the tribe of Naphtali. Through all of Scripture, there is not one unkind word about the fallow deer. Rather, it is the frequent image of grace and beauty. Coupled to these images of visual delight, the fallow deer also assumes a symbol of philosophic delight, a symbol of freedom.

We find both these visual and philosophic relationships in the lyrical beauty of the Song of Songs: "My beloved is like . . . a young hart: behold, he standeth behind our wall, he looketh forth at the windows, shewing himself through the lattice" (Song of Songs 2:9). And: "Until the day break, and the shadows flee away, turn, my beloved, and be thou like . . . a young hart upon the mountains of Bether" (Song of Songs 2:17).

Singing a song of thanksgiving after his victory over the Philistines, David indulged in a little vanity, saying of God: "He maketh my feet like hinds' feet: and setteth me upon my high places" (II Samuel 22:34).

Habbakuk exalts the joy of salvation by echoing David's praise. Again, the fallow deer becomes the image of ethereal freedom: "The Lord God is my strength, and he will make my feet like hinds' feet, and he will make me to walk upon mine high places" (Habbakuk 3:19).

The wisdom of Solomon extended the beauty of the fallow deer in a simile that likened it to the beauty of morality. Preaching marital fidelity, the King called on his people to remain loyal to their spouses and to refuse any temptations that would lead them toward a breach of that faith. Of a married woman, the wise Solomon said, "Let her be as the loving hind" (Proverbs 5:19), that gentle animal that avoids reckless adventures and immoral behavior.

The fallow deer was considered a clean animal (Deuteronomy 14:5) and, despite his obvious admiration for it, was frequently included on Solomon's banquet table (I Kings 4:24).

The destruction of habitat and centuries of aggressive hunting have all but extirpated the fallow deer in the Middle East. The common fallow deer was saved by man and for centuries has been kept as a specimen of beauty in zoos, parks, and private estates around the world. The Mesopotamian fallow deer, however, has not done so well. Indeed, it was thought to be extinct until only about a hundred years ago when a small herd of them was found along the Karkheh River, in the remote Khuzestan region of Iran. Only a few dozen of these animals still live there today.

The Israeli Hai Bar Society and the Holy Land Conservation Fund have been working hard for many years to obtain a few of these fallow deer in order to start a small breeding herd at Hai Bar North, a reserve area in northern Israel. If this can be done, the deer will be encouraged to breed within the highly protected confines of their ancient habitat. And when enough have been bred, to ensure the survival of the species, individuals will be turned loose into the wild to inhabit areas they had not known for ten or fifteen centuries.

Many of these areas in northern Israel are well suited for the reintroduction of the Mesopotamian fallow deer because through the past three decades an extensive effort has been made to reforest large areas that are now capable of supporting a healthy population of the species.

When that day arrives, many conservationists will understand the joy that Isaiah expressed when he contemplated the day when "the ransomed of the Lord shall return, and come to Zion with songs and everlasting joy upon their heads" (Isaiah

35:10). On that day, the prophet said, "Then shall the lame man leap as an hart" (Isaiah 35:6).

It is the fallow deer, chosen by David as an image of salvation, that inspired the psalmist to write: "As the hart panteth after the water brooks, so panteth my soul after thee, O God" (Psalms 42:1).

DOGS

"Yea, they are greedy dogs which can never have enough"   (ISAIAH 56:11)

THE DOG is a worthless cur; a surly, shameless scavenger. Despised and tormented, the domestic dog (*Canis familiaris*) is pelted by a continuous stream of abuse all through Scripture.

This animal, which earned the popular reputation as "man's best friend," didn't start its association with the human community with such high esteem. Even today, while there is a relatively warm relationship between man and dog, our language is salted with phrases of contempt in which the dog is the symbol of disrepute. And most of this derogation is rooted deeply in the Scripture of all three monotheistic religions.

To call someone a "dog" is to suggest he is vile and despised. So it was in the days of ancient Egypt, when Moses was told of the terrible punishment that was waiting for the

Pharaoh's henchmen who had persecuted the captive Hebrews: "But against any of the children of Israel shall not a dog move his tongue, against man or beast: that ye may know how that the Lord doth put a difference between the Egyptians and Israel" (Exodus 11:7).

Today we have phrases "go to the dogs" or "throw to the dogs," meaning to be ruined or sacrificed to an unworthy beneficiary. There are also interesting scriptural passages that indicate these phrases are much older than the English language. When the prophet Elijah cursed King Ahab to a degrading death, he said, "Thus saith the Lord, In the place where dogs licked the blood of Naboth shall dogs lick thy blood, even thine" (I Kings 21:19). And David, decrying the banality of those who attacked him, complained: "For dogs have compassed me: the assembly of the wicked have inclosed me: they

pierced my hands and my feet" (Psalms 22:16). In this last case, we might even say David's tormentors "hounded" him, adding another verb of derogation to our canine-linked vocabulary.

Digging deeper, we find the roots of English phrases such as "die a dog's death," "dogs of war," "let sleeping dogs lie," and the miserably hot "dog days" of summer all part of Scripture.

The dog became the symbol of perfidious hypocrites in all three monotheistic religions. Jewish Scripture claims paganism as the ultimate folly and likens the unfaithful who return to heathen ways to dogs: "As a dog returneth to his vomit, so a fool returneth to his folly" (Proverbs 26:11).

This concept was picked up in Christian Scripture by the apostle Peter in his admonishment of those converts who turned away from Christianity: "For it had been better for them not to have known the way of righteousness, than, after they have known it, to turn from the holy commandment delivered unto them. But it is happened unto them according to the true proverb, The dog is turned to his own vomit again" (II Peter 2:21–22).

Islam also equates the dog and the hypocrite: "but he clung to the earth and followed his own lust. Therefore his likeness is the likeness of a dog; . . . Such is the likeness of the people who deny Our revelation" (Surah 7: Al A'raf:176).

Islamic contempt for the dog is deeply woven into the fabric of that religion. For a Moslem, a dog is filth and anything touched by a dog must be purified before it can be used again. If a dog drinks from a water vessel, that vessel must be cleansed seven times, including one good scouring with sand, before a human may use it again. Dogs must not be permitted near Moslem worshipers, since the animal's presence automatically makes any prayer worthless. Angels will not enter a building that houses a dog, and even the prophet Mohammed had to perform a purification ritual over a place where a dog had slept before the Angel Gabriel would appear to reveal a mystery of the Koran to him.

Even so, the Moslem sage Al Sindi once commented, "Allah does not create anything in which there is not a trace of his wisdom." Thus, there is a place for the dog in the Moslem world, and this place is as a hunter. Bedouin tribesmen for centuries have kept a particular breed of Persian greyhound commonly called seluki to hunt gazelle. But the hunting must conform to criteria set in the Koran, which includes certain training requirements as well as a command that the hunter must cry out *Bismillahi illahi Akbar!* (In the name of God, the great God!) before the hunting dogs are unleashed (Surah 5: Al Ma'idah:4).

In Scripture, to call oneself a "dog" is to speak with great humility: "And he bowed himself, and said, What is thy servant, that thou shouldest look upon such a dead dog as I am?" (II Samuel 9:8) and "she said, Truth, Lord: yet the dogs eat of the crumbs which fall from their masters' table" (Matthew 15:27).

And to call someone else a "dog" is to speak with great contempt: "But now they that are younger than I have me in derision, whose fathers I would have disdained to have set with the dogs of my flock" (Job 30:1). Here also we find some evidence that dogs were used for shepherd duty. Job, it should be remembered, was known as a wealthy man who counted most of his estate in livestock, and he most probably used dogs to help tend many of these animals.

David used a dog simile in describing the political gossips of his day: "They return at evening: they make a noise like a dog, and go round about the city" (Psalms 59:6).

Calling someone a "dog" may also suggest he is prone toward being dilatory: "His watchmen are blind: they are all ignorant, they are all dumb dogs, they cannot bark; sleeping, lying down, loving to slumber" (Isaiah 56:10).

When the wandering Hebrew tribes made a prohibition against pagan practices, the dog became synonymous with male temple prostitutes: "Thou shalt not bring the hire of a whore, or the price of a dog, into the house of the Lord thy God for any vow: for even both these are abomination unto the Lord thy God" (Deuteronomy 23:18).

The image of the dog improves somewhat when we read Gideon's defeat of the Midianite armies. The Israelite general needed three hundred reliable soldiers from a population of ten thousand, and a little divine advice helped him make the selection: "So he brought down the people unto the water: and the Lord said unto Gideon, Every one that lappeth of the water with his tongue, as a dog lappeth, him shalt thou set by himself; likewise every one that boweth down upon his knees to drink" (Judges 7:5). Gideon counted out the three hundred men who lapped water as dogs, organized his striking force, and crushed the Midianites.

The Hebrew word for dog is *kelev*, stemming from an onomatopoeic verb meaning "to bark." The Arabic name for the dog, *kalb*, stems from the same Semitic root; this word is also used by Moslems as a slang name of disrespect for Christians.

The dog, quite possibly, was the first animal to be domesticated by man, and is the only member of the Canidae family to truly tolerate domestication. Other close relatives include the wolf, jackal, and fox, species of which all exist in the Middle East. Many zoologists believe that the dog is actually a part of the wolf genus and that all dogs are direct descendants of ancient species of wolves.

Several breeds of pariah dog were common in the land of Scripture, but most were exterminated early in this century during the British Palestine Mandate's antirabies campaigns. The seluki maintains a firm popularity among the Bedouin, and several Israeli kennels are concentrating on breeding the pariah dog of Canaan.

DOVES

"Oh that I had wings like a dove!"   (PSALMS 55:6)

THE DOVE is life.

The dove (family Columbidae) assumes many symbolic meanings through Scripture, some approaching the greatest aspirations of humanity, but still there is only one symbol with which the dove is totally identified—life.

On a primary level, the dove is the symbol of biological life. It is the annual harbinger of spring recalled by Solomon: "The flowers appear on the earth; the time of the singing of birds is come, and the voice of the turtle [dove] is heard in our land" (Song of Songs 2:12). Here the dove symbolizes a rejuvenated world growing in the warmth of spring, a new beginning for life.

With the story of the Flood, the dove becomes a more abstract symbol of life. "And again he [Noah] sent forth the dove out of the ark; And the dove came in to him in the evening; and, lo, in her mouth was an olive leaf plucked off: so Noah knew that the waters were abated from off the earth" (Genesis 8:10–11).

This first postdiluvian springtime was more symbolic than the annual passage of seasons because it was also the rebirth of a world purged of wickedness. If the Flood is understood as the judgment of an angry God on a corrupted humanity, then the salvation of Noah and his family represents the compassion of God to make covenant with the righteous. The symbol of this covenant to life, the deliverance from the lethal waters of the Flood, is the dove. It is the dove, bearing the simple olive leaf, that proclaims the revival of a world cleansed of wickedness, that proclaims the salvation of the deserving,

that proclaims life.

Christian Scripture extends the life symbolism of the dove into a purely spiritual interpretation. As John baptized Christ, "the Holy Ghost descended in a bodily shape like a dove upon him, and a voice came from heaven, which said, Thou art my beloved Son; in thee I am well pleased" (Luke 3:22). As baptism is a ceremony symbolic of spiritual purification, the few drops of water John sprinkled on Christ may be viewed as the spiritual equivalent of the Flood. And as the dove of physical life announced a cleansed world to Noah, so a dove of spiritual life announced a cleansed world of spirit to Christ.

Thus, the dove maintains its image as the proclaimer of life through this series of three scriptural passages, each progressing into greater abstraction. However, the concept of life symbolized by the dove is constant. Only the interpretations of life become more profoundly abstract.

The dove is also a symbol of many of life's higher aspirations—peace, purity, godliness, sensitivity, and freedom. Just as the dove returned to Noah proclaiming renewed peace between God and man, the dove has become a universal symbol of peace between man and man. When Jesus commissioned his apostles to preach the Christian gospel, they were instructed to approach humanity cautiously and in the spirit of peace: "Behold, I send you forth as sheep into the midst of wolves: be ye therefore wise as serpents, and harmless as doves" (Matthew 10:16).

This concept is carried from an earlier time when David, a thousand years before Christ, pleaded with God: "O deliver not the soul of thy turtledove unto the multitude of the wicked: forget not the congregation of thy poor for ever" (Psalms 74:19).

The symbol of the dove being the antipathy of wickedness, violence, and corruption is echoed many times through Scripture. This is noticed particularly in passages that portray the conflict between the corruption of man-made society and the purity of God-made nature.

Praying to God for deliverance from oppression, David cries: "Oh that I had wings like a dove! for then would I fly away, and be at rest. Lo, then would I wander far off, and remain in the wilderness. Selah" (Psalms 55:6–7).

Predicting the divine judgment of Moab, the prophet Jeremiah pleaded: "O ye that dwell in Moab, leave the cities, and dwell in the rock, and be like the dove that maketh her nest in the sides of the hole's mouth" (Jeremiah 48:28).

Those who survive the social punishments of war, pestilence, and famine will be those who flee social life and live as ascetics: "But they that escape of them shall escape, and shall be on the mountains like doves of the valleys, all of them mourning, every one for his iniquity" (Ezekiel 7:16).

Ezekiel's image is quite appropriate for the idea he wanted to set in his reader's mind. Surely, the dove has the ability to fly and escape, but it also makes a gentle, murmuring call; the voice of a dove is a plainting sound, almost a mourning call. The concept of mourning, however, suggests the recognition of privation, a recognition of wrongdoing, for without this, there can be no repentance. This thought is expressed by Isaiah: "I did mourn as a dove: mine eyes fail with looking upward: O

Lord, I am oppressed; undertake for me" (Isaiah 38:14).

Man does not seek only to escape the oppression of his fellowman, but also from the sometimes harsh commandment of God. In Hebrew the word for dove is *jonah*, and the entire Book of Jonah may be interpreted as a metaphor in which the plight of a peaceable dove seeks to flee from the burdening commands of God. Jonah's attempt at escape was, of course, unsuccessful. And after his experience with the sea monster, he fulfilled the commandment of God by preaching to the hostile Assyrians in Nineveh. Reverting to symbolism, the picture is clear: Jonah, the dove, is free to escape the onerous taxes of mankind, but cannot escape the rule of the universe, the command of God.

Three types of doves are still common in the lands of Scripture: the turtle dove, the palm dove, and the rock dove. Indeed, the turtle dove and the palm dove have survived well and have spread across almost all the warm areas of Asia, Africa, and Europe. But it is the hardy rock dove that has best adapted itself to the changing world. This species has many varieties, the most common of which can be seen from Manhattan to Peking and is known as the common pigeon.

All doves are considered clean birds and good eating by Jews, Christians, and Moslems alike, and are even listed specifically as acceptable food under the dietary laws of kosher.

But somehow, the sale of doves as food seems to be among the more loathsome of professions. The gospel writers tell of Christ's distress when encountering dove sellers in the Temple of Jerusalem on Palm Sunday: "And Jesus went into the temple of God, and cast out all them that sold and bought in the temple, and overthrew the tables of the moneychangers, and the seats of them that sold doves, and said unto them, It is written, My house shall be called the house of prayer; but ye have made it a den of thieves" (Matthew 21:12–13).

On a more human level, the dove is a symbol of physical beauty. In the great dialogue of conjugal love, we read: "His eyes are as the eyes of doves by the rivers of waters, washed with milk, and fitly set" (Song of Songs 5:12). Continued use of this symbolism develops the image to passages of great beauty and literary value.

Perhaps one of the most eloquent tributes to the common housewife was written by the psalmist three thousand years ago: "Though ye have lien among the pots, yet shall ye be as the wings of a dove covered with silver, and her feathers with yellow gold" (Psalms 68:13).

EAGLES

". . . exalt thyself as the eagle" (OBADIAH 4)

"T HE WAY of an eagle in the air" (Proverbs 30:19) is a wonder set beyond the understanding of a wise man.

What strange and wonderful power could keep such a magnificent bird aloft, gliding as an angel, almost too high for earthbound man to see? What fantastic power could bring this bird to plummet thousands of feet, as a bolt of lightning, only to swoop low, strike its prey, and then be off again into the thinness of the mountain air?

The mystery of the airborne eagle is the mystery of an amazing and terrific power. And it is no wonder that the eagle, in Scripture, becomes the image of tremendous power, the image of the two strongest and constantly conflicting forces of the universe, the image of good and the image of evil.

This wondrous power of the eagle, to seemingly defy natural forces that anchor man to the earth, is likened to the power of God. Explaining to Moses that the Israelites have become the Chosen People, God reminds the great leader: "Ye have seen what I did unto the Egyptians, and how I bare you on eagles' wings, and brought you unto myself" (Exodus 19:4). Likewise, this great power is the strength of God protecting a single, reverent man: "As an eagle stirreth up her nest, fluttereth over her young, spreadeth abroad her wings, taketh them, beareth them on her wings: So the Lord alone did lead him [Jacob], and there was no strange god with him" (Deuteronomy 32:11–12).

In Christian theology the eagle assumes a similar symbolism, and is sometimes used as the image of Christ protecting early Christian believers from the depradatious evils of the world: "And when the dragons saw that he was cast unto the

earth, he persecuted the woman which brought forth the man child. And to the woman were given two wings of a great eagle, that she might fly" (Revelation 12:13–14).

As the eagle is the symbol of divine protection, it is also the image of protection for the divine—a sort of palace guard, as it were. The prophet Ezekiel records an inspiring vision of the heavenly throne. Before the seat of universal power stood four beasts standing guard. The prophet describes them, commenting: "they four also had the face of an eagle. Thus were their faces: and their wings were stretched upward; two wings of every one were joined one to another, and two covered their bodies" (Ezekiel 1:10–11).

In Christian revelation, St. John, traditionally known as The Divine, had a similar vision, and again, the four beasts were evident before the powerful throne. One of these beasts was "like a flying eagle. And the four beasts had each of them six wings about them" (Revelation 4:7–8).

On occasion, divine power is conferred to selected humans: "But they that wait upon the Lord shall renew their strength; they shall mount up with wings as eagles; they shall run, and not be weary; and they shall walk, and not faint" (Isaiah 40:31). Again, the power of eagles also can be granted to specific individuals. Eulogizing the recently slain King Saul and his son Jonathan, victims of a battle with the Philistines, David recalls that they "were lovely and pleasant in their lives, and in their death they were not divided: they were swifter than eagles" (II Samuel 1:23).

While the eagle is frequently the symbol of divine strength and the power of virtue, it is also used as a symbol for pagan aggression. Paradoxically, the eagle that protects the godly is also the eagle that enflames the pagans. Habakkuk, prophesizing the Chaldean invasion, warns: "they shall fly as the eagle that hasteth to eat" (Habakkuk 1:8).

Prophesizing divine judgment of the pagan Edomites, inhabitants of the mountainous areas southeast of Israel, Jeremiah charged: "Thy terribleness hath deceived thee, and the pride of thine heart, O thou that dwellest in the clefts of the rock, that holdest the height of the hill: though thou shouldest make thy nest as high as the eagle, I will bring thee down from thence, saith the Lord" (Jeremiah 49:16).

Obadiah saw the similarity between the powerful, mountain-dwelling eagles and the hostile inhabitants of the Edomite mountains: "Though thou exalt thyself as the eagle, and though thou set thy nest among the stars, thence will I bring thee down, saith the Lord" (Obadiah: 4).

In all of these cases, Jewish and Christian alike, it appears as if the "eagle" written into the English translation is not a true eagle at all, but rather the griffon vulture (*Gypaetus fulvus*), a spectacular bird that was once very common in the Middle East.

The original Hebrew version of the Bible calls the great bird *nesher*, a name that stems from a verb meaning "to tear apart." This suggests a vulture, and a passage from the prophet Micha seems to confirm the identification: "Make thee bald, and poll thee for thy delicate children; enlarge thy baldness as the eagle [*nesher*]" (Micah 1:16). Commenting on the baldness of the nesher strongly suggests the white-headed griffon. No other bird in the Middle East so accurately accepts this identity. Christian scholars also tend to agree that the "eagle" of the New Testament is none other than the Hebrew *nesher*, the griffon vulture.

Other religions and cultures add evidence to corroborate this identification. The Koran records that there was a pagan eagle-god, Nasr: "And they [doomed pagans] have said: Forsake not your gods; Forsake not . . . Nasr" (Surah 71: Noah:23). Here it appears that the Hebrew *nesher* and Arabic *nasr* stem from the same Semitic root.

To the north, the griffon-headed god of Assyria, Nisroch, became that nation's symbol of military strength. Again, it appears to be the same bird, the mighty griffon vulture. Nisroch later was adopted as the military standard of the Persian Empire, and subsequently was seen atop the standards of the Roman legions.

The Roman griffon was prophesized centuries before Romulus and Remus founded their mighty city on the Tiber: "The Lord shall bring a nation against thee from afar, from the end of the earth, as swift as the eagle [*nesher*] flieth; a nation whose tongue thou shalt not understand" (Deuteronomy 28:49).

The *nesher*, which is used as the symbol of amazing rescues and awesome power, is an imposing bird. A century ago, the naturalist H. B. Tristram, who was surveying the flora and fauna of Palestine commented, "It is unfortunate that our language has only one word 'Vulture' for the noble griffon." Taken by the magnificence of the great bird, Tristram slipped into prose of acclaim, and possibly exaggeration, in what is otherwise an unflavored and decidedly scientific study. After observing many griffons soaring over Wadi Kelt, just west of Jericho, Tristram commented, "It is impossible in any part of the country to look up without seeing some of them majestically soaring at an immense height."

This is the same extraordinary bird that inspired Job to write: "Doth the eagle mount up at thy command, and make her nest on high? She dwelleth and abideth on the rock, upon the crag of the rock and the strong place. From thence she seeketh the prey, and her eyes behold afar off. Her young ones also suck up blood: and where the slain are, there is she" (Job 39:27–30).

David, who also had a leaning toward being a naturalist, observed the griffon's molt, and included it in the Psalms: "Who satisfieth thy mouth with good things; so that thy youth is renewed like the eagle's" (Psalms 103:5).

Even Jesus Christ made an ornithological observation, commenting on the griffon's carrion diet. Warning his followers of false phophets who preach for personal gain, Christ said: "For wheresoever the carcase is, there will the eagles be gathered together" (Matthew 24:28).

While the griffon is the most spectacular vulture of the Middle East, other species have been observed and recorded in Scripture. One such vulture is the *peres*, or bearded vulture (*Gypaetus barbatus*). Although the English name refers to the bird's tufted chin, the Hebrew name has quite another meaning. *Peres* stems from the verb "to break" and alludes to this vulture's habit of seizing live prey, carrying it to great heights, and dropping it thousands of feet to break apart on jagged rocks below.

The Egyptian vulture (*Neophron percnopterus*) is known in Hebrew as the *racham*, a name that is derived from the verb "to love." This apparently ironic name for a vulture was probably chosen because of the great affection and care it shows for its young. The Egyptian vulture also has one other characteristic that sets it well apart from its feathered peers. It is the only bird of prey known to use tools. Ornithologists have documented how the Egyptian vulture picks up rocks in its beak and throws them at ostrich eggs in order to break their tough shells.

There are, incidentally, a few true eagles in the Middle East. But these relatives of the griffon vulture are considerably smaller in size, relatively rare, and of much less significance in Scripture.

FISH

"And makest men as the fishes of the sea" (HABAKKUK 1:14)

THE FIRST DISCIPLES of Christ were fishermen. He gathered them one day, nearly twenty centuries ago, along a beach of the Sea of Galilee. Walking along the sandy shore outside the village of Capernaum, Jesus probably noticed all the construction a few miles to the south where Herod Antipas was building a magnificent new city in honor of his Roman Emperor, Tiberias. But Christ chose to stay near the small fishing village to find his first followers.

St. Matthew records that day when Christ approached the edge of the water and "saw two brethren, Simon called Peter, and Andrew his brother, casting a net into the sea: for they were fishers. And he saith unto them, Follow me, and I will make you fishers of men. And they straightway left their nets, and followed him" (Matthew 4:18–20).

The trio walked farther down the beach and encountered two more brothers, James and John, sons of Zebedee, mending their fishing nets. Again, Christ called, and the two new apostles responded.

From this beginning, Christ built a discipleship that would spread around the world, developing into one of mankind's great monotheistic faiths. And it became a faith that reflected its origins—Jewish law modified by liberal Greek thought, and, of course, its simple origins beside a small fishing village.

Just as the Star of David and the menora developed into symbols of Jewish culture, and the crescent moon and towering minarets symbolize Islam, the Christians also adopted symbols: the crucifix and the fish. Indeed, by a curious coincidence, the ancient Greek word for fish, "ΙΧβΥΣ," soon became an acronym for "Ιησος Χιρστος βεου Υιος Σωτηρ," translated to "Jesus

Christ, Son of God, Saviour."

The fish became a major symbol in Christian Scripture as well. In fact, the entire New Testament has been viewed through the metaphor of a great, spiritual fishing expedition.

Matthew, who was also from Capernaum, saw strong religious symbolism in the livelihood of the village: "Again, the kingdom of heaven is like unto a net, that was cast into the sea, and gathered of every kind: Which, when it was full, they drew to shore, and sat down, and gathered the good into vessels, but cast the bad away" (Matthew 13:47–48).

Episodes concerning fish and fishing are threaded through the New Testament, some stories holding profound symbolic thought and others simply relating events in Christ's ministry.

Fish figured into several of Christ's miracles during the days he preached to the crowds of the Galilee area. One of the better known miracles was the Passover meal that he fed to five thousand followers. It consisted only of "five barley loaves, and two small fishes" (John 6:9).

More symbolic was the miraculous draft of fishes. Climbing into a boat with his apostles, Christ instructed Peter: "Launch out into the deep, and let down your nets for a draught" (Luke 5:4).

On their Lord's instructions, the apostles started to work. And their toils were so successful that the great catch of fish threatened to sink the two boats engaged in the netting. Christ saw their anxiety and said: "Fear not; from henceforth thou shalt catch men" (Luke 5:10).

While Christ commissioned his fishermen apostles to use the skills of their trade in their ministry to the world, fishing also helped pay the taxes. Confronted with the tax collector, Jesus instructed Peter: "Notwithstanding, lest we should offend them, go thou to the sea, and cast an hook, and take up the fish that first cometh up; and when thou has opened his mouth, thou shalt find a piece of money: that take, and give unto them for me and thee" (Matthew 17:27).

The Christians by no means have a monopoly on scriptural fish. Islamic literature makes reference to the sea in the description of Creation: "And He it is Who hath constrained the sea to be of service that ye eat fresh meat [fish] from thence, and bring forth from thence ornaments which ye wear" (Surah 16: An-Nahl:14).

There is also a koranic parable about a fishing village that did not keep the Sabbath as a day of worship: "how they did break the sabbath, how their big fish came unto them visibly upon their sabbath day . . . thus did We try them for, that they were evil-livers" (Surah 7: Al A'raf:16).

The ancient Israelite community held the fish in mild disdain. True, the fish was permitted to be eaten (Leviticus 11:9), and fish were imported to Jerusalem as a staple food (Nehemiah 13:16) to the extent that one of the city's gates eventually earned the name "Fish Gate." But the fish was also a pagan god of the Philistines, the hated enemies of the Israelites. In one battle the Philistines captured the Israelite ark of the convenant and set it before their fish-god Dagon: "And when they of Ashdod arose early on the morrow, behold, Dagon was fallen upon his face to the earth before the ark of the Lord" (I Samuel 5:3).

Incidentally, this is a good point to note the close similarities of those early Semitic languages. The Hebrew word for fish is *dag*, stemming from a verb meaning "very prolific." The Philistines, being a coastal people dependent to some extent on the sea, worshiped the fish-god Dagon, whose name stems from the same root.

It is quite possibly because their mortal enemies held the fish in such reverence that the Israelites generally disdained the aquatic species. In Hebraic Scripture, the fish is often a symbol of ignorance: "For man also knoweth not his time: as the fishes that are taken in an evil net" (Ecclesiastes 9:12).

Habakkuk, lamenting a nihilistic greediness in humanity, used the fish as an image for the victims of treachery: "And makest men as the fishes of the sea . . . that have no ruler over them? They take up all of them with the angle, they catch them in their net, and gather them in their drag: therefore they rejoice and are glad. Therefore they sacrifice unto their net, and burn incense unto their drag; because by them their portion is fat, and their meat plenteous" (Habakkuk 1:14–16).

The "great fish" that swallowed Jonah is perhaps the best known of scriptural fish: "Now the Lord had prepared a great fish to swallow up Jonah. And Jonah was in the belly of the fish three days and three nights" (Jonah 1:17). From inside this great fish, the doughty Jonah repented to God: "And the Lord spake unto the fish, and it vomited out Jonah upon the dry land" (Jonah 2:10).

In this episode the fish reaches its greatest symbolism in Jewish Scripture, acting as an instrument of God to exact repentance and obedience from a resisting man.

It was prophesized that the first warning of the destruction of Jerusalem would come via the Fish Gate: "And it shall come to pass in that day, saith the Lord, that there shall be the noise of a cry from the fish gate, and an howling from the second, and a great crashing from the hills" (Zephaniah 1:10).

Several varieties of fish are still taken from the waters in and around the Holy Land. Carp, which are traditionally part of Jewish cooking, are raised in ponds in northern Israel. The St. Peter's fish, named for the first apostle and former fisherman, is a common catch in the Sea of Galilee. Indeed, this freshwater fish most probably was Peter's main catch before Christ called him to join his "fishers of men."

FOXES

"Take us the foxes, the little foxes" (SONG OF SONGS 2:15)

SHY, yet inquisitive; gentle, yet violent; small, yet powerful; and also capable of outwitting a dozen men, the fox is among the most brilliant of all animals in the lands of Scripture.

And tenacious, too!

Where entire civilizations have been dislodged from the ancient city of Jerusalem, the fox (*Vulpes vulpes*) has "outfoxed" them all, holding on, with amazing stamina, to the grand city in the Judean hills.

Quite possibly, the fox should be the symbol of Jerusalem, for it is the one animal, man included, that has stayed with the city through both days of greatness and days of desolation.

When Jerusalem was at the height of its grandeur, during the days of Solomon, the fox was common to the scene. It was so common that gardeners spent hours, usually unsuccessfully, trying to keep the fox from their ripened vineyards: "Take us the foxes, the little foxes, that spoil the vines: for our vines have tender grapes" (Song of Songs 2:15).

Although this is a metaphor, and the fox is a symbol for those who would spoil the sweet fruit of Solomon's love, we can be sure the real fox was the perfect image for this verse and was continuously scouting the neighborhood, ready to raid a vineyard or fig orchard at any opportunity.

But the greatness of Solomon's Jerusalem did not last. A few centuries later it was destroyed, and its people carried to Babylon. Yet the fox survived and remained with the emptied city. Jeremiah recorded the event: "the mountain of Zion, which is desolate, the foxes walk upon it" (Lamentations 5:18).

When the Israelites were released, they returned to their city and found foxes to greet them. There is a biblical story about Nehemiah, returning from Nebuchadnezzar's Babylon, to rebuild the walls of Jerusalem. He was met by a scornful cynic, an Ammonite named Tobiah, who ridiculed the idea of feeble and recently humbled Jews rebuilding their city: "Even that which they build," Tobiah said, "if a fox go up, he shall even break down their stone wall" (Nehemiah 4:3).

It seems certain that Tobiah was alluding to the fox's small stature and lack of brute force, suggesting the Jews didn't have the strength to rebuild a city that could withstand even the smallest intruder.

Of course, Tobiah was wrong. The walls were rebuilt, and it took many centuries before they were to crumble again. And it took more brute force than that of a mere fox—it took the legions of Rome.

And Tobiah was wrong in his observations of the fox. True, the small animal is not the image of physical power, but it more than compensates for this through its cunning intelligence. Biblically, the fox's cunning is considered a symbol of untruth. As a fox might use devious means because of his lack of physical power, so false prophets may be devious when not possessing true spiritual power: "O Israel, thy prophets are like the foxes in the deserts" (Ezekiel 13:4).

Christ, journeying to Jerusalem, was warned by the Pharisees to change his plans or Herod Antipas would have him killed. Replying, Christ compared the Roman's tetrarch to a malicious fox: "And he [Christ] said unto them, Go ye, and tell that fox, Behold, I cast out devils" (Luke 13:32).

Unlike most wild animals, the fox is normally monogamous, frequently mates for life, and usually keeps a permanent den—even though it's a mere hole in the ground. Christ recognized this and commented to a scribe volunteering to become one of his disciples of hard times that may lie ahead: "The foxes have holes . . . but the Son of man hath not where to lay his head" (Matthew 8:20).

In some episodes of Scripture, there appears a confusion between the small and crafty fox and its larger relative the jackal. Seeking vengeance on the Philistines, "Samson went and caught three hundred foxes, and took firebrands, and turned tail to tail, and put a firebrand in the midst between two tails" (Judges 15:4). Then Samson turned these burning animals loose into the Philistine grain fields, and in their panic they spread the fire through the growing food.

While this may be considered by many as a terrible means of attaining vindictiveness—using cruelty to animals to satisfy a passion for vindictiveness—it is quite unlikely Samson actually used foxes for the exploit. More likely, he used jackals. Simply, it would have been a monumental feat even beyond the power of Samson to catch three hundred foxes for the job. Jackals, on the other hand, would have been more available and much easier to catch.

Also, David, wandering the Judean Desert, cried out against those who sought to destroy him: "They shall fall by the sword: they shall be a portion for foxes" (Psalms 63:10). Again, the animal probably meant was the jackal, the Middle East's most notorious scavenger.

The fox is a good hunter. Although he has a bad reputa-

tion for raiding gardens with sweet fruits, and occasionally infiltrating a flock of domestic fowl in search of a meal, he is also extremely skilled at hunting in the wild. Extraordinary hearing, sense of smell and eyesight, as well as the fox's uncanny facility for stalking prey, help the small mammal master the hunt and thwart his predators. Although foxes do well hunting birds, mice, and other similar animals, they also have a reputation for taking rather large and powerful snakes, as well as the lethal scorpion.

As in the days of Solomon, and through the various destructions and reconstructions of Jerusalem, the tenacious fox is still very much an inhabitant of the area, and an active population still causes concern among farmers when the grapes in their vineyards begin to ripen.

GAZELLES

". . . as swift as the roes upon the mountains" (1 CHRONICLES 12:8)

THE GAZELLE is a creature of supple beauty. Soft and light, it is a pure image of gentleness and grace.

The ancient Hebrews named this animal *zvi*, a word that means "glorious," and, indeed, the gazelle is a glorious animal. It is a fleet-flooted antelope that normally avoids contact with the human community. Thus, in Scripture, we often find it used as a symbol for a distant predilection. It is the symbol of a passion so often chased, and so rarely captured.

The elusive gazelle is inaccurately translated as "roe" in English Bibles. This is most likely because the medieval English scribes of King James's court didn't know what a gazelle was, so they used their name of a distant cousin that inhabits northern European forests. Their only firsthand accounts of the fleeting gazelle were from the often-distorted journals of the Crusaders, those knights on armored horses who were no match for the swift symbol of beauty.

Indeed, this swiftness has long been part of the lore of the land of Israel. And the same speed that eluded the Crusaders bounds through the Song of Songs: "behold, he cometh leaping upon the mountains, skipping upon the hills. My beloved is like a roe" (Song of Songs 2:8–9).

The free beauty of the gazelle was so rooted in the minds of the Israelites that it was occasionally used as the substance of an oath: "I charge you, O ye daughters of Jerusalem, by the roes . . . of the field, that ye stir not up, nor awake my love, till he please" (Song of Songs 2:7).

The gazelle's characteristic caution is proverbially symbolic. It is the core of an idea that suggests that beauty possessed is beauty destroyed: "Deliver thyself as a roe from the hand of the hunter" (Proverbs 6:5). This passage implies that just as the seeking hunter will destroy the beauty of the gazelle at the end of the chase, so any beauty possessed by the covetous will perish, for a key element of beauty is freedom.

Although the gazelle is among the most delicate of creatures, it is also an animal of substantial speed, capable of running with a bounding stride with speeds in excess of forty miles per hour: "and were as swift as the roes upon the mountains" (I Chronicles 12:8). Attributing this swiftness to a human was a great compliment: "and Asahel was as light of foot as a wild roe" (II Samuel 2:18).

The fleetness of the gazelle attains its greatest symbolic value in describing those who would seek to avoid the ultimate apprehension—divine judgment: "Therefore I will shake the heavens, and the earth shall remove out of her place, in the wrath of the Lord of hosts, and in the day of his fierce anger. And it shall be as the chased roe . . . they shall every man turn to his own people, and flee every one into his own land" (Isaiah 13:13–14).

The glory of the gazelle, or *zvi*, attains its greatest symbolic value in the description of Jerusalem's Mount Zion as the "glorious holy mountain," or in Hebrew, *har zvi kodesh*: "And he shall plant the tabernacles of his palace between the seas in the glorious holy mountain" (Daniel 11:45). The phrase *har zvi kodesh* might also mean "holy Mount Gazelle," for this seat of David's capital, where the tabernacles were set within the citadel between the Dead Sea and the Mediterranean, was frequented by gazelles all through ancient times and up to the nineteenth century.

Our English word "gazelle" comes from the Arabic *ghazal*, which denotes the same animal. And as in Hebrew, the Islamic symbolism for this creature is one of paramount beauty.

In Moslem tradition, it is the lustrous eyes of the gazelle that are the image of supreme beauty; it is the most beautiful part of the most beautiful creature. The soft gaze of the gazelle is likened to "an ebony pupil set in ivory," and often becomes a symbol for the beauties of Paradise in the Koran: "And we shall wed them [the Moslem elect] unto fair ones with wide, lovely eyes" (Surah 44: Ad-Dukhan:54).

Arabs kept gazelles as sacred animals at Tabala and Mecca, and one tribe, Harith, held the genus in such high regard that whenever a dead gazelle was found by a member of the tribe, it had to be washed and buried with respectable ceremony. And then the entire tribe went into mourning for seven days

Commonly known as *bint al-raml* ("daughter of the sand"), the gazelle is a classical image in Arabic literature. The *ghazal* is also the name for a form of Arabic poetry dedicated to love songs.

For all the beauty represented by the gazelle in Middle Eastern culture, it is ironic that several species are on the verge of man-made extinction. Soldiers of both Israeli and Arab armies once took great sport in hunting gazelles with their long-range automatic weapons. Today, this is generally forbidden, particularly in Israel, where the gazelle population is protected by law.

Bedouin hunters still use a traditional combination of falcons and dogs in hunting gazelles. A trained falcon is set

aloft to find the gazelle and attack it, pecking out its eyes. Specially trained seluki hunting dogs are then unleashed to run down the blinded animal and kill it.

Only a century ago, the naturalist H. B. Tristram observed that dorcas gazelles were "extremely common in every part of the country south of Lebanon, and the only large game which is really abundant." Today, the dorcas (*Gazella dorcas*) is an endangered species, extirpated in most of the Middle East and extremely rare in its few remaining habitats.

GOATS

"And if his offering be a goat, then he shall offer it before the Lord" (LEVITICUS 3:12)

P ITY THE domestic goat. No other animal in all creation seems chosen to carry such an enormous portion of humanity's burden. The functions demanded of the goat are many; his rewards are few.

Possibly the first animal to be domesticated by man, the goat has served both physical and spiritual needs of his human masters for millenniums. A constant servant of early man, the goat was slaughtered to provide food for his family, and sacrificed as an offering to God.

Spiritually, the goat is nearly synonymous with sacrifice. Mentioned several times in the Torah, the goat assumed a dual role of mortal sacrifice and living atonement. From the days of the Hebrew patriarchs, the goat had been sacrificed as a sin offering before the altar of God: ". . . he shall bring his offering, a kid of the goats, a female without blemish, for his sin offering, and slay the sin offering in the place of the burnt offering" (Leviticus 4:28–29).

Aside from mortal sacrifice, the goat also became the central figure of another religious ceremony of the ancient Hebrews, the outcasting of the scapegoat. Described in the Torah, the patriarch Aaron brought a goat before the tabernacle of the congregation: "And Aaron shall lay both his hands upon the head of the live goat, and confess over him all the iniquities of the children of Israel, and all their transgressions in all their sins, putting them upon the head of the goat, and shall send him away by the hand of a fit man into the wilderness" (Leviticus 16:21).

Thus, in this dual role of mortal sacrifice and living atonement, the goat soon found itself a cornerstone of the evolving monotheism of the Hebrews. While sister tribes among the early Semites were still offering human sacrifice, the Hebrews developed the concept of symbolism. Therefore, the sacrifice and the atonement of the scapegoat were merely symbols of a worship that, in reality, was abstract. The God worshiped was metaphysical, incorporeal, and incapable of being defined in terms of the physical world.

Yet man was a physical being, and the simpler men had difficulty relating to their God on purely abstract terms, so an intermediary, a symbol, had to be introduced. And this intermediary was, in many cases, the goat.

After the Hebrews had established themselves as a nation with a fixed land, there was a tendency to abandon the symbolic practices of the desert and make the direct spiritual link between man and God. The prophet Isaiah was encouraged by this trend, and wrote: "To what purpose is the multitude of your sacrifices unto me? saith the Lord . . . I delight not in the blood of bullocks, or of lambs, or of he goats" (Isaiah 1:11). The prophet then suggested a more humanistic course: "Learn to do well; seek judgment, relieve the oppressed, judge the fatherless, plead for the widow" (Isaiah 1:17).

In his epistle to the Hebrews, the apostle Paul used images his readers knew well, images they had known from Isaiah. In explaining some of the abstract precepts of Christianity, Paul wrote: "it is not possible that the blood of bulls and of goats should take away sins" (Hebrews 10:4).

Paul also uses Judaic terms in this epistle to extend the blood sacrifice concept in explaining the crucifixion of Christ: "Neither by the blood of goats and calves, but by his own blood he entered in once into the holy place, having obtained eternal redemption for us" (Hebrews 9:12).

The goat was destined for more than spiritual sacrifices in the Old Testament, and we find it slain also to hide the acts of a crime. Part of Joseph's destiny was to be sold into slavery by his brothers. In order to hide their treacherous act, "they took Joseph's coat, and killed a kid of the goats, and dipped the coat in the blood" (Genesis 37:31). Joseph's father, Jacob, was shown the coat and was convinced his son had been killed by a wild beast, thereby remaining passively behind to let his enslaved son continue to fulfill the destiny that would decide the foundations of the twelve tribes of Israel.

While the goat held important spiritual significance to the early Hebrews, it was also of great economic importance. Fitting into the general scheme of nomadic life in the Middle East, the goat is well adapted to forage among the sparse grasses and thorns that cling to the fringe of the desert.

Today's Bedouin tend goats in much the same manner as the Hebrews of four thousand years ago. Goat hair is woven into curtains and tent covers; goat skins are fashioned into various leather goods, from soft sandals to great water bags. Goat milk and cheese have long been favorites of the desert nomad, even from the days of Solomon: "And thou shalt have goats' milk enough for thy food, for the food of thy household, and for the maintenance for thy maidens" (Proverbs 27:27).

And, of course, goat meat was accepted as clean under the laws of kosher (Deuteronomy 14:4).

The manifold uses of the goat possibly made many of the early Hebrews ponder man's relationship to that animal. In

their early probings of morality, those Hebrews even afforded a semblance of justice to their goats in the law: "Thou shalt not seethe a kid in his mother's milk" (Deuteronomy 14:21). This has since been expanded to include all animals, and the strict divisions between meat and dairy dishes is a mark of all kosher kitchens.

Although the goat has been domesticated for untold centuries, the Bible makes a division between domestic and wild goats, a division that views the wild mountain goat as a symbol of gentle freedom in the wilderness, while the domestic goat developed as the image of a humble, sacrificial servant.

In several instances, domestic goats are likened to human qualities. Jeremiah, telling of the Israelite escape from the Babylonian captivity, used goats as a symbol for leadership: "Remove out of the midst of Babylon, and go forth out of the land of the Chaldeans, and be as the he goats before the flocks" (Jeremiah 50:8).

Perhaps more poetic is the use of goats in the simile of the Song of Songs: "Behold, thou art fair, my love . . . thy hair is as a flock of goats, that appear from mount Gilead" (Song of Songs 4:1).

As the goat has served humbly from the early pages of Genesis and all through Scripture without giving the slightest indication of being evil, it is ironic that the goat is used as a symbol of the damned in the Christian version of the Day of Judgment: "And before him shall be gathered all nations: and he shall separate them one from another, as a shepherd divideth his sheep from the goats: And he shall set the sheep on his right hand, but the goats on the left. Then shall the King say unto them on his right hand, Come, ye blessed of my Father, inherit the kingdom prepared for you from the foundation of the world" (Matthew 25:32–34).

What's to become of the goats? A few verses later we find out: "Then shall he say also unto them on the left hand, Depart from me, ye cursed, into everlasting fire, prepared for the devil and his angels" (Matthew 25:41).

Humble to the last, the goat bears the heaviest of burdens to eternity.

HORSES

". . . horses that the kings of Judah had given to the sun" (II KINGS 23:11)

LONG BEFORE THE Hebrew tribes had even started their wanderings in the desert, horse hooves thundered under the command of human riders across the great steppe of Russia.

One of the first animals to be domesticated by man, the horse (*Equus caballus orientalis*) quickly developed to become a symbol of great power and wealth. Horses became the pets of kings at a time when the sport of kings was war.

The military value of horses was quickly learned. It was fast and powerful, and when properly trained, was one of the few animals that would charge into the heat of a battle.

It didn't take long for the ancient Egyptian pharaohs to recognize this useful animal, and they quickly added cavalry units and chariots to their armies. Even when Egypt was gripped by a seven-year famine, Pharaoh kept building stables, multiplying his horses, and feeding them the precious grain that otherwise could have helped feed a starving population. Money had failed, and a barter system was reestablished. People could trade their belongings for some of the grain Pharaoh had stored away: "and Joseph gave them bread in exchange for horses" (Genesis 47:17).

During the years that the Hebrews lived in Egyptian slavery, Pharaoh kept building his cavalry, and when it pleased him, he would send out the swift and thundering horse soldiers to terrorize his captive Jews.

The torment became insufferable, and Moses was hard pressed to lead his people away, to follow the commission of God that ordered him to bring the harassed Hebrews to the Promised Land of Israel. But Pharaoh refused to let them leave. Moses was then instructed by God to take a firmer stand before Pharaoh and tell him: "Let my people go. . . . Behold, the hand of the Lord is . . . upon the horses . . . there shall be a very grievous murrain" (Exodus 9:1, 3).

But neither this nor a series of plagues sent by God softened Pharaoh's stand. The situation worsened, and Moses became compelled to take action. In the darkness of night, Moses broke Pharaoh's law and moved his 600,000 Hebrews out of Egypt to begin their forty years of wandering in the desert.

When Pharaoh discovered this, he quickly mobilized his army: "But the Egyptians pursued after them, all the horses and chariots of Pharaoh, and his horsemen, and his army, and overtook them encamping by the sea" (Exodus 14:9).

The powerful Egyptian horses could have easily trampled the defenseless Hebrews had it not been for a miracle. God parted the seas and opened a path through which Moses led his people into the Sinai Desert. But the Egyptians pursued even here, with the cavalry and chariots violently threatening the fleeing Hebrews. Another miracle saved the day—God sent a great pillar of fire against the Egyptians, forcing them back from Sinai and into the path cleared through the parted sea. But before the Egyptians could get back to the Egyptian side, God let the water surge back to its original space "and covered the chariots, and the horsemen, and all the host of Pharaoh" (Exodus 14:28).

Free from the Pharaoh and his terrifying horse army, the Hebrews adopted new laws that would guide their lives and their leaders. One law was: "But he shall not multiply horses to himself, nor cause the people to return to Egypt, to the end that he should multiply horses: forasmuch as the Lord hath said unto you, Ye shall henceforth return no more this way" (Deuteronomy 17:16).

Reentering the Promised Land, the Hebrews had little use for horses anyway, with little inclination toward raising the great animals whose only major use seemed to be for warfare. The Hebrews were a pastoral people who could ill afford to keep animals that weren't economically productive. Horseflesh was not clean food; horses produced neither milk nor wool. They were not as powerful as the ox when it came to pulling a plough. In fact, the only civil use for a horse seemed to be as a means of rapid transportation, but the Hebrews could only move as fast as their herds of sheep and goats.

In time, however, the Hebrew tribes became settled. They gave up their nomadic wanderings and started to build permanent communities. With the establishment of these settlements, they found a need for rapid communication and an army to defend their cities. They started to raise horses.

By the time of Solomon, Israel had become a great power, and the horse, that terrifying weapon the Egyptians had used in their persecutions, started to become common in the land of Israel: "And Solomon gathered together chariots and horsemen: and he had a thousand and four hundred chariots, and twelve thousand horsemen" (I Kings 10:26).

The demand for horses had become so great that Solomon broke the ancient law: "And they brought unto Solomon horses out of Egypt, and out of all lands" (II Chronicles 9:28).

By the time of Josiah, the horse became a most highly prized animal; too high, according to the King. Josiah erupted

with a sweeping program of reform, and in one measure "he took away the horses that the kings of Judah had given to the sun" (II Kings 23:11). The horse would not become a temple animal for pagan gods.

In one episode of the Bible, a horse literally ran to the rescue of Israel. During the time of the Persians, the pagan nobleman Haman had ordered the extermination of the Jews. Esther, a Jewish maiden, had become the Queen of Xerxes, and learned of the evil plot against her people. She pleaded with the King to stop Haman and let her people live in peace. The King, known to the Israelites as Ahasuerus, agreed and appointed Mordechai to draft an order countermanding the evil Haman's designs: "And he wrote in the king Ahasuerus' name, and sealed it with the king's ring, and sent letters by posts on horseback" (Esther 8:10). The swift horses reached Haman before he could start his attacks, and the Israelites were saved from the Persian sword.

The event is remembered in the Jewish festival of Purim.

More often, however, the horse is not running to a rescue. Rather, it is dispatched with its rider on an errand of violence. In the Koran, an entire Surah is devoted to the horses of war. The first seven lines portray a vivid image of a band of mounted brigands sweeping out of the desert on a raid at dawn: "By the snorting coursers Striking sparks of fire, And scouring to the raid at dawn, Thus, therewith, with their tail of dust, Cleaving, as one, the center of the foe, Lo! man is ingrate unto his Lord And lo! in the love of wealth he is violent" (Surah 100: Al A'adiyah:1–7).

The horse is one of the few animals that can be trained to charge blindly into a battle, and, perhaps because of this, it is often considered stupid: "Be ye not as the horse . . . which have no understanding, whose mouth must be held in with bit and bridle, lest they come near unto thee" (Psalms 32:9). And: "A whip for the horse, a bridle for the ass, and a rod for the fool's back" (Proverbs 26:3).

Horses are still popular animals in the Middle East today. The famed Arabian horses are a familiar breed known for their grace, speed, and ability to adapt to rigorous training. Aside from being kept by many wealthy Arabs, they are also common among Arab military units, but mostly as ornamental or ceremonial animals. In Israel horses are used as work animals on kibbutzim and other agricultural communities. Horses are also used for patrol duty around some nature reserves, particularly during the rainy season when motor vehicles tend to get stuck and bogged down in the mud when they're driven off the road.

Remember Solomon's passion for horses and chariots? Here's a verse that would make any girl swoon: "I have compared thee, O my love, to a company of horses in Pharaoh's chariots" (Song of Songs 1:9).

HYENAS

"Mine heritage is unto me as a speckled bird" (JEREMIAH 12:9)

A PIERCING, hysterical laugh cuts the predawn darkness of the Judean desert. Men and beasts awake with a start.

Then a long and mournful wail splits the night, echoing eerily up and down the steep-walled wadi. Another shrieking laugh shatters the stillness, an insidiously terrifying laugh that sounds like the ravings of a madman.

But is is not a madman. The Bedouin of the desert know this cry, and the superstition of centuries sends them springing to their feet, grabbing weapons, and dashing outside their goat-skin tents with fearful apprehensions. The men start to secure the livestock. Mothers stuff plugs into their children's ears, and do the same to themselves to shut out the voice of evil. Each member of the family stays within sight of another.

No one among the Bedouin believes the Westerner's theory that the hyena is a shy and timid creature. Westerners do not live with the beast. The Bedouin know that the hyena is plagued with madness. They have seen it digging up graves, exhuming human bodies. They know it will snatch a goat or a young lamb, or even an infant, if it gets a chance. They know its hypnotic cry will lure an unwary man into its lair, and there he will be devoured in a vicious onslaught.

The hyena is referred to very few times in Scripture, and only once is it mentioned specifically. And to show how little Westerners know of this terrible beast, it's translated wrongly as a "speckled bird." The fearful prophet Jeremiah saw a belligerent world around him and cried: "Mine heritage is unto me as a speckled bird [*ayit tsavua*], the birds round about are against her; come ye, assemble all the beasts of the field, come to devour" (Jeremiah 12:9).

Ayit tsavua is translated by most contemporary scholars as a hyena, and in this light the prophet's words paint a demoniacal scene of death in the desert. Fate brings the victim to the hyena's mesmerizing plaint and a heinously terrible death. As the hyena feeds on the victim, the "birds round about"—the vultures circling the scene—prepare to consume what the hyena can't gourge into its stomach. Soon, all the scavengers of the desert move in to clean up whatever scraps are left.

While *ayit tsavua* means "camouflaged bird" in contemporary Hebrew, most scholars agree the biblical meaning is substantially different. Generally, scholars agree, *ayit tsavua* meant "rapacious animal" to the ancient Israelites. And most agree that this animal is the striped hyena (*Hyaena hyaena striata*).

This theory is strengthened by a lesson in biblical geography. There are two places in the Bible with the name "Zeboim," which is a derivative of the Hebrew *tsvauim*, the plural of *tsvua*—in short, places believed to be named for the hyena.

The first mention is of a town named Zeboim that belonged to the tribe of Benjamin (Nehemiah 11:34). If there was a Benjaminite town named for the hyena, it should have been situated in the eastern part of the tribe's territory, in the Judean desert near Jericho, one of the striped hyena's favorite habitats.

Then, an episode of Scripture gives us another clue. During King Saul's wars with the Philistines, much fighting took place in the Benjaminite lands north and east of Jerusalem. Scripture tells of a three-pronged Philistine attack on Saul's headquarters at Gilbeah, the Israelite encampment about three miles north of Jerusalem: "one company turned unto the way that leadeth to Ophrah, unto the land of Shual: And another company turned the way to Beth-horon: and another company turned to the way of the borders that looketh to the valley of Zeboim toward the wilderness" (I Samuel 13:17–18).

Looking at a map, we can trace the Philistine attack and also tentatively locate the "valley of Zeboim," the valley of hyenas. The first company mentioned attacked from Ophrah, the ruins of which are known today as being about ten miles north of the Israelite stronghold at Gilbeah. The second company's assault came from Beth-horon, which archaeologists have identified as having been about ten miles northwest of Gilbeah.

Now we come to the third assault force. They attacked after making a turn that brought them near a border from which the valley of Zeboim could be viewed in a wilderness setting. Since the Philistine force must have marched north and eastward from their homeland to take up positions at Ophrah and Beth-horon, it seems reasonable that the third company, in making its turn, would have been approaching Gilbeah from the far side, from the east. This is the only approach left, because they could not have approached from the south without passing near Jerusalem, where they might have been seen and an alert passed on to King Saul.

Also, to the east, there is a "way of the border"—the Jordan River—the border that has divided the Middle East for uncounted centuries.

Looking toward the site of Gilbeah from the Jordan, there

is only one major valley leading up from the wilderness. It is a valley today known as Wadi Kelt. Logically, this is the vale that was once known as the valley of Zeboim.

A visit to the area today shows it hasn't changed much since the Philistines marched along its serpentine floor in their assault on Gilbeah. It is a barren and rugged valley that was once the home of hermits. Bedouin tribesmen pass by the area in their nomadic wanderings, and sometimes stop for a while in late spring and early summer, when a little grass lingers on area hilltops to feed their flocks of goats and sheep, and herds of camels. By September the entire region is again lifeless—except for the predators that hide among the rocks and the hyenas that live in the caves.

While hunting and antirabies campaigns have exter-minated most of the hyena in Israel, the species still inhabits the area around Wadi Kelt. Its nocturnal cries and howls still bring fear to the Bedouin nearby.

By most standards, the striped hyena is a grotesque animal. Anatomy hasn't favored it with grace or speed. Rather, it ambles with an awkward gait which restricts most possibilities of chasing down game. Consequently, it often turns to scavenging. Its strong front paws are good for unearthing buried carrion, and its powerful jaws can crush the bones of any animal inhabiting the Middle East. But despite Bedouin superstitions, most zoologists consider the hyena as a retiring animal that normally runs away as soon as it detects the presence of man. The hypnotic effect of its voice is also disclaimed by most zoologists.

IBEX

"The high hills are a refuge for the wild goats"   (PSALMS 104:18)

THE CONCEPT OF refuge—safety from danger, troubles, and oppression—is a common theme in Scripture. In a very real sense, each of the three major monotheistic religions went through periods of mortal danger at the times of their sacred writings, and each sought refuge from those who would harm them because of their beliefs.

The Koran is well seasoned with the bitter herbs of oppressions and persecution suffered by the first men who accepted Al Islam. Indeed, the start of the Islamic era is measured from June 20, 622 C.E., the date when Mohammed and his followers flew to refuge at Al-Madinah. The first Christians likewise suffered blood for their faith. The list of martyrs attests to their sacrifices and longing for shelter.

One of the most endearing of scriptural passages dealing with the concept of refuge is found in Jewish Scripture. It occurred when the young shepherd boy David had slain the giant Philistine, Goliath, in a battle. The feat brought the youth great popularity, and the Israelite King Saul grew terribly jealous—so jealous that he plotted to kill the boy whose greatest delight was composing psalms of praise to God. When David learned of the King's evil plot, he ran to a refuge "in strong holds at En-gedi" (I Samuel 23:29).

In English "En-gedi" means "Spring of the Young Goat." It is an oasis, deep in the Judean desert, named after the rare Nubian ibex (*Capra ibex nubiana*), a striking species of mountain goat that inhabits the area.

To the naturalist, the Nubian ibex and En-gedi are nearly synonymous. These nimble animals have inhabited the lush oasis since before the dawn of history. They thrived amid a profusion of exotic flora, mountain springs, and magnificent waterfalls in a pristine and idyllic setting.

The Nubian ibex and En-gedi are synonymous to the religious philosopher also. Both have become symbols of refuge, images of peace and security surrounded by a hostile world. En-gedi has long been the locale favored by many recluses, refugees, and exiles. And the Nubian ibex is the symbol incarnate of En-gedi.

Centuries before the Israelite tribes entered the Promised Land, the ibex wandered the cliffs and craggy outcroppings around the oasis, watching humanity take its first steps toward civilization. In these Chalcolithic times, immediately after man turned his back on the darkness of the Stone Age, a human community organized at En-gedi, building a social structure and agreeing on a form of leadership. These early people started to work with man's first metal, copper, and one of the images they fashioned was that of their constant companion at the oasis, the Nubian ibex.

Chalcolithic artifacts found by archaeologist Pessah Bar Adon in the nearby Mishmar Valley included a scepter crowned with the images of the Nubian ibex. In this instance, Bar Adon believes the ibex stood as the symbol of fertility to the early society. Fertility was one of the prime concepts of these early people, a concept that on a broader scale means enduring strength; thus it crowned the scepter, the symbol of a ruler's power.

The symbol chosen by this ancient civilization was extraordinarily perceptive. The Nubian ibex survived the Chalcolithic era, and centuries after the primal culture vanished, these hardy mountain goats endured.

The ibex watched the wandering Israelites as they entered the Land of Canaan, and perhaps a few watched from too close, and found they were included as edible meat under the new dietary laws of kosher (Deuteronomy 14:5).

For centuries, the oasis of En-gedi remained on the periphery of Israelite occupation. It was a place distant from the great cities, a place where refugees, such as David, could hide in safety.

Reading David's psalms, we find a good picture of what this refuge must have meant: "From the end of the earth will I cry unto thee, when my heart is overwhelmed: lead me to the rock that is higher than I. For thou has been a shelter for me, and a strong tower from the enemy" (Psalms 61:2–3). The high rock, the strong tower, assuredly suggest David envisioned the mighty cliffs that surrounded En-gedi as being symbolic of divine protection.

Later in the Psalms, we meet the image again: "The high hills are a refuge for the wild goats" (Psalms 104:18). And surely, they are. These hills rise steeply from a base at the shore of the Dead Sea, and ascend more than a thousand feet with stark precipices that defy all but the most adept and nimble creatures.

While David found En-gedi a good refuge when he was in fear for his life, his son and successor to the throne, King Solomon, found the enchanting beauty of the oasis, at the base of these cliffs, a refuge from the burdens of kingship. Solomon was so impressed by this home of the Nubian ibex that it was included in his great song of nuptial love: "My beloved is unto me as a cluster of camphire in the vineyards of En-gedi" (Song of Songs 1:14).

The ibex of En-gedi served as more than a consummate

biblical image and an occasional meal for the early Israelites. It also physically entered into the religious ceremony at the great temple of Jerusalem. Each year at Rosh Hashanah, the Jewish New Year, a "shofar," or horn, is traditionally blown in Jerusalem at the site of the Temple. Customarily, this horn is fashioned from the great sweeping horns of the Nubian ibex. Symbolically, the ibex helps usher in the new year and helps to proclaim the hope—indeed, the refuge—Jews seek in the new calendar.

The progression of centuries saw the land of Israel swept by a great succession of invasions. Through each of these invasions, the ibex watched from their lofty cliffs, surveying the changing world beneath them. They inhabited En-gedi while Assyrian and Babylonian invasions marched through the land. During the reign of Jehoshaphat, the ibex watched foreign armies try a back-door assault on Jerusalem, from the oasis of En-gedi. And they watched those armies retreat after being crushed by the waiting Israelites.

The ruins around En-gedi testify to what the ibex had witnessed. Evidence of the intrusions of Rome, Persia, Byzantium, and Islam still stands in various states of decay, half covered by the vegetation that draws its life from the "Spring of the Young Goat." Through each assault, the ibex clung to its image of survival in refuge. While the nearly constant progression of wars through the Middle East have exterminated several species of wildlife, it is a grand providence that the Nubian ibex still lives in its remote refuge.

The Hebrews name for the ibex, *ya'el*, and the Arabic, *wa'l*, mean the same thing, "to ascend." This has been the main reason for the ibex's survival. Shy, suspicious, and nimble,

these animals can avoid most predators, even the occasional leopards that wander through, by scampering up the steep faces of the area's cliffs. This agility is with the ibex almost from birth, and even the well-practiced rock climbing of Bedouin poachers is not enough for them to catch an ibex more than two days old.

One of the few things an ibex can't outrun in the rocky outcroppings of its refuge is a rifle bullet. For this reason, the twentieth century has brought the species to the verge of extinction. Hunters, seeking tasty meat or the spectacular, crescent-shaped horns of the male ibex, decimated the formerly stable population. Until recently, there was a real fear that one of the more splendid beasts of creation would be exterminated forever.

Then, in 1965, the Nubian ibex received legal protection from the Israeli government, and a strong conservation effort coaxed the shattered herd toward recovery. En-gedi itself was named a nature reserve area and the Israeli Nature Reserves Authority devised a plan to rescue the endangered species.

Avraham Yoffe, director of the Reserves Authority, deputized the most skilled wildlife handlers in the area—the Bedouin poachers—and put them to work rounding up infant goats within hours of their birth. The kids were carefully nurtured and received complete protection in a compound built in the Negev Desert. Here they grew and started breeding among themselves. In time, there were enough ibex so that some could be reintroduced to several areas of Israel, to fortify the dwindling numbers that were clinging tenaciously to their rocky ancestral home.

The project worked, and today, the Nubian ibex is no

longer considered an endangered species. The rescue is one of the few bright spots in a century that has brought extinction to more wildlife species than any other time before.

Today, at En-gedi, the ibex are as wild and free as they ever were. There are no fences keeping them in, yet they hold to the area as if it had some strange magnetic power. They can prove to be an enigma today as they had so many centuries ago when they were used in a metaphor that illustrated the limited capacity of human knowledge. Speaking from a whirlwind, God asked Job if he could influence the stars, or if he perceived the breadth of the earth, or even if he knew "the time when the wild goats of the rock bring forth" (Job 39:1).

Job couldn't answer. Even today, as man does reach for the stars, and measures every corner of the earth, the Nubian ibex of En-gedi still remains a mystery with the aura of freedom within refuge, with an aloofness that remains above the notoriously shifting human community.

The Nubian ibex is a symbol of a certain timelessness, something that survives despite the world, and because of the world. It is a rare and beautiful creature, with beauty so striking that three thousand years ago, Hebrew slang called a beautiful woman *ya'el* (Proverbs 5:19).

And just as that unknown Chalcolithic ruler of six thousand years ago contemplated the enduring strength of these children of the wilderness and used its image on his own scepter of enduring strength, so today the Israeli Nature Reserves Authority has adopted the same image as its seal and symbol for the preservation of wildlife in the lands of Scripture.

JACKALS

"I will make a wailing like the dragons" (MICAH 1:8)

WHEN WE READ a passage from the Bible such as "And Hazor shall be a dwelling for dragons, and a desolation for ever" (Jeremiah 49:33), we quickly perceive a reflection from remote antiquity. There is a vision of vast distances in time and space that sets the passage in a fabulous realm which seems more the product of imagination than of history. Hazor, that great city of the north which fell before Nebuchadnezzar's sword twenty-five centuries ago, and dragons, those fierce and cunning beasts of mythology, give the passage an obscure aura of incredibility.

Yet the passage is pure truth, and not just truth in an idealistic aspect. It is truth as valid as any historical account of any event in human records. For sure, there was a Hazor; and for sure, there was the *tan*, the animal translated in English as dragon.

The translators would have been a bit more accurate had they translated *tan* as "jackal." This is the name of the jackal in contemporary Hebrew, and this is most probably the name by which the ancient Israelites knew the species.

Reading the Bible in this light, many passages begin to make more sense. And when we become aware of the jackal's characteristic habits—its gregarious nature, carrion diet, nighttime howling, and scavenging around the ruins of human communities—the significance of these passages becomes even more clear.

Thus, when the prophet pleads to God: "Behold, the noise of the bruit [report] is come, and a great commotion out of the north country, to make the cities of Judah desolate, and a den of dragons" (Jeremiah 10:22), we get a vivid image of the turmoil spreading through the Judean cities, of the appre-

hension that grips a country threatened with invasion. We understand through the use of the "dragon," or jackal, as a symbol, that the invader means to destroy the Judean cities and turn them into ruins where the jackals can scavenge at will —and not just a stray jackal, but a whole den, a whole family, connotating that they will replace the human families that once inhabited those communities.

Through Scripture, the jackal symbolizes hardship, retribution, and destruction. It is a fierce creature that thrives on human calamity. The greatest punishment God could deliver to the wayward Israelite tribes was the destruction of the heart of their lands—Jerusalem. And even this was threatened: "And I will make Jerusalem heaps, and a den of dragons" (Jeremiah 9:11). Again, describing the ruins as the habitation of a den of jackals suggests the destruction will be complete.

The vision of a den is important here because a jackal will prowl the edges, and sometimes penetrate into, communities inhabited by humans. But he won't build his den there. The den where jackal pups are raised is invariably away from human habitations.

The voice of the jackal is a mournful howl. To this day, the nocturnal howling of the jackal is relatively common through the Middle East, just as it was centuries ago when Micha, lamenting the sins of Israel, cried: "I will wail and howl, I will go stripped and naked: I will make a wailing like the dragons" (Micha 1:8).

Job, bemoaning his own misfortunes, lamented, "I am a brother to dragons" (Job 30:29), and in so few words wrapped up the whole concept of his personal catastrophe; his world was ruined, his misfortunes were complete, he had nothing left but the rubble of former happiness. Job became kin to jackals, and like jackals, he was relegated to live in the wake of disaster, scavenging on the debris of past affluence.

The home of the jackal is desolation, and only destruction awaits those who enter there. With a note of bitter irony, Isaiah prophesized: "And the wild beasts of the islands shall cry in their desolate houses, and dragons in their pleasant palaces" (Isaiah 13:22). Here we have a prophesy of the fate of Babylon.

Isaiah becomes more specific in describing the judgment of the archenemies of Zion: "And thorns shall come up in her palaces, nettles and brambles in the fortresses thereof: and it shall be an habitation of dragons" (Isaiah 34:13).

While the place of the jackals is a place of mortal danger, the promise of divine protection is a strong shield against these fearsome beasts: "the young lion and the dragon shalt thou trample under feet" (Psalms 91:13).

The English translators of the Bible fell into an understandable confusion with the jackal. The plural Hebrew noun meaning jackals is *tannim*, a word that was easily confused with the Hebrew singular noun meaning sea monster, *tannin*. Consequently, both were translated as "dragons," since the early-seventeenth-century English could envision no other creature with powers so broad that it could ravage through the ruins of desert cities as well as violently churn the oceans into a tempest. Today, reading the King James Version of the Bible, we simply have to decide at each passage whether our "dragon" is terrestrial or aquatic.

If it's a land animal, then it's a jackal. In many ways, the literary symbolism manifest in the jackal is accurate. All the howling, scavenging, and gregariousness is quite true. But, unfortunately, this leaves us with a rather limited picture of the jackal. True, this close cousin of the domestic dog feeds on carrion, but it is also a rather resourceful hunter, working cooperatively in packs that seek and share prey. True, the jackal inhabits ruins, but it doesn't create them. Most of the ruins inhabited by jackals are the destruction of an even more violent species—man. Actually, the jackal is a rather shy animal and prefers ruins only because the humans have already left.

The Syrian jackal (*Canis aureus syriaca*) is the species common to the Middle East, where its numbers have been considerably reduced in rabies control programs this century. This species, however, is not in danger of extinction and is still frequently heard, if not seen, in many areas.

LEOPARDS (CHEETAHS)

". . . a leopard shall watch over their cities" (JEREMIAH 5:6)

NATURE MAKES its own balances. For years we have been hearing that the first law of nature is the survival of the fittest, but this is not so. The first law of nature is the survival of nature, and not necessarily the most powerful or most adaptable individual species.

A good example of nature working to protect itself is in the remarkable discovery of the Sinai leopard, an animal that was thought to be extinct for centuries.

Back·in the 1960s, the Israeli Nature Reserves Authority worked hard to save an endangered mountain goat called the Nubian ibex. Intensive hunting and the devastation of frequent wars had all but exterminated the gentle species around its ancestoral habitat of En-gedi, a small oasis on the western shore of the Dead Sea.

Careful protection of the ibex, along with a strong effort to build a breeding herd, resulted in the rescue of the species. In fact, the endangered animal responded so well to this encouragement that it made a surprising revival and now roams the rocky cliffs around En-gedi in great numbers.

But whenever one species starts to become too numerous for its habitat, nature often introduces a predator. And to keep the Nubian ibex from overrunning the oasis, nature brought back its ancient foe, the Sinai leopard.

There had been rumors that the rare leopard had been in the area for some time. Bedouin, those nomadic desert dwellers, had made reports of seeing leopards in the more remote quarters of the Judean desert. In 1970, when the ibex were starting to make their comeback at En-gedi, footprints that surely appeared to be those of a leopard were found nearby.

Naturalists had set out meat, mostly animals that had been killed by automobiles, in an attempt to lure the leopard into a positive sighting. Then, in the fall of 1974, all the work paid off.

A group of naturalists found an ibex in the cliffs near En-gedi. It was dead, and appeared to be the victim of a great cat. Figuring that the cat would return that night to feed on its kill, the naturalists set up blinds near the carcass and sat patiently with their cameras ready.

The cat did return for its waiting supper and provided the naturalists with the first photographs ever taken of the rare Sinai leopard. It returned as if ordered by nature to help maintain the living balance at En-gedi and preserve the oasis' fragile ecosystem.

Incidentally, the appearance of the leopard to devour the young mountain goat that it had killed also proved that the world has not yet reached the peaceable kingdom envisioned by the prophet Isaiah where "the leopard shall lie down with the kid" (Isaiah 11:6).

In Scripture, it seems that the ancient Hebrew word *namer*, meaning "spotted," was used to identify both the leopard (*Panthera pardus*) and the cheetah (*Acinonyx jubatus*), both of which inhabited the area during biblical times. English translations of the Bible refer to leopards only.

At the close of biblical times, it appears that the Israelites also developed a separate name for the cheetah, a word that, ironically, may be the basis for our word "leopard." The ancient Israelites called the cheetah *bardeles*, which may be the root for the ancient Greek *pardus*, which was followed by the later Greek *leopardus* and subsequently by the English "leopard."

In the Bible the leopard is the symbol of violent revenge. Prophesizing the destruction of hypocrites in Israel, Jeremiah said, "a leopard shall watch over their cities: every one that goeth out thence shall be torn in pieces: because their transgressions are many, and their backslidings are increased" (Jeremiah 5:6).

The image of the leopard is precise. Jeremiah chose the most brutal animal that he could have known. No other cat seems to delight in lethal bloodletting as much as the leopard. It is not a predator with a lightning strike, nor does it fall on its prey with a ponderous and crushing blow. Rather, the leopard attacks with a steady mauling action, destroying its victim piece by piece in a protracted and grueling fight.

Leopards are not particularly large cats, at least when compared to lions and tigers. But they do tip the scales at a respectable 175 pounds, and every ounce of this is pure strength. Pound for pound, the leopard is the strongest cat alive.

Two other attributes of the leopard make it well suited for En-gedi and keeping the ibex population in check. First, it is a good climber, capable of bounding up the thousand-foot cliffs that tower above the oasis with greater skill than any other predator in the region. This is particularly important for an animal that hunts a prey as nimble as a mountain goat.

Second, the leopard has great stealth. It has neither the awesome power of a lion nor the swift striking speed of the cheetah, and so must rely on its ability to move in absolute silence as it stalks its wary prey.

The Bible also uses the leopard as a symbol for the immutable, as an image of something that cannot change. This appears in one popular metaphor that explains that confirmed evil can never become good: "Can the Ethiopian change his skin, or the leopard his spots? then may ye also do good, that are accustomed to do evil" (Jeremiah 13:23).

Leopards had a wide range in the lands of Scripture, and were most frequently found in the northern mountains of ancient Israel: "look from the top of Amana, from the top of Shenir and Hermon . . . from the mountains of the leopards" (Song of Songs 4:8).

Since the sighting of the Sinai leopard in the Judean desert, naturalists have surmised that there may be about a half dozen of the animals still alive in their ancient homeland. There is great hope that they may now increase in numbers as they help reestablish the balance of nature in the area. If this happens, the hope continues that they may someday be reintroduced to the northern mountains, to the "mountains of the leopards."

Zoologists have not yet been able to study the Sinai leopard closely and are not sure if the Sinai leopard is a distinct species or a subspecies. And this academic point might not be learned for a long time, because the Nature Reserves Authority has no intention of trying to catch any of the great beasts. Their plan is to leave the great cat where it belongs, in its natural environment. None will be taken for study or for zoos.

The cheetah is a distant feline cousin of the leopard and is best known for its amazing speed.

Habakkuk, writing of the sweeping invasion of the Chaldeans, who carried the Israelites off into Babylonian captivity, was probably referring to the cheetah when he wrote: "Their horses . . . are swifter than the leopards" (Habakkuk 1:8). The cheetah, which favors the flat plains and broad, open valleys, is the perfect image of speed. It can launch itself into a sprint that peaks at speeds in excess of seventy miles per hour, making this cat the fastest animal on the face of the earth.

Speed is not the only characteristic that makes the cheetah a unique cat. Called *fahd* in Arabic, the cheetah is one of the few big cats that can be trained by man. For centuries, Arab dignitaries have kept trained cheetahs as symbols of wealth and as aristocratic hunting animals.

The hunting cheetah is a very special animal. First, only cheetahs born in the wild will do. They must be captured as adolescents, after their parents have taught them to stalk and strike. Then a long and difficult training period teaches the cheetah to respond to human commands. The cat must integrate its instincts—youthful education in the wild and loyalty to its human master.

Once trained, the cheetah is among the most efficient of hunting animals. Unleashed, the cheetah finds and strikes down its prey with a lightning attack, swiftly and efficiently dealing a lethal blow. The cheetah is the least brutal of any cat and takes its prey with an almost merciful strike.

This type of attack is characteristic of the cheetah in the wild as well. Since it is substantially smaller than most big cats, the cheetah must rely more on skill than might. Its long straight legs give it an extremely fast speed that compensates considerably for its lack of brute strength. Its nonretractable claws, unique among cats, give it tremendous traction and turning ability, which also helps with its lightning attack. When it reaches its prey, after using much energy in its running attack, the cheetah must make a near instantaneous kill. It usually has little energy left to put up much of a fight. Thus, it normally lunges at the back of its prey's neck, delivering an almost surgical blow to snap the spinal column and kill its victim.

Although the leopard and cheetah may seem quite similar when you first look at them in a zoo, they are among the most diverse of cats. They are different in temperament, habitat, agility, and anatomy. A close inspection of the spotted coat of each cat will show them quite different in this respect, too. The cheetah has solid black spots, while the leopard's are somewhat circular.

The leopard enters Christian tradition at the apocalypse: "And I stood upon the sand of the sea, and saw a beast rise up out of the sea . . . and upon his heads the name of blasphemy. And the beast which I saw was like unto a leopard" (Revelation 13:1–2).

What beast came from across the sea with the crushing force of a leopard? What beast brought blasphemy on its shield and the mauling onslaught that ravaged the land? The image seems to be that of ancient Rome, which, under Emperor Titus in the year 70 C.E., destroyed the ancient Israeli kingdom and mutilated the holy city of Jerusalem.

LEVIATHANS

". . . the great dragon that lieth in the midst of his rivers" (EZEKIEL 29:3)

T ERRIFYING SEA MONSTERS lurked in the turgid waters of antiquity. They were great demons, deadly creatures that would crush and devour any foolhardy land animal that stumbled into the aquatic realm.

It seems quite natural that the ancient Hebrews viewed the mysteries of the deep with awe and suspicion. They were desert people, nomads that wandered a burning and waterless territory. For these people of arid lands, great waters meant only one thing—evil. It was the great flood that destroyed the world of their ancestors. The Philistines, or "sea peoples," were among their worst enemies. And when the ancient Israelites were twice held in slavery, it was beside great rivers, the Nile of Egypt and the Euphrates of Babylon. Even during the days of the great King Solomon, Israel was not much of a maritime power.

The ancient Hebrews had little use for great waters. Simple wells and springs were adequate for them and their livestock. Consequently, they never made any extensive study of sea creatures; such beasts could only mean vexation and trouble. So it is no wonder that when we meet water beasts in the Bible, they are the image of malevolence.

Two of the most gruesome and frightening water monsters of the Bible are the leviathan and tannin. These denizens of the watery world are shrouded in the same enigmatic obscurity as their aquatic habitat. Today, we simply can't be sure exactly what the writers of Scripture meant when they wrote "leviathan" or "tannin."

The identification of these water creatures is difficult and is only complicated by modern Hebrew. Today, the word "leviathan" means "whale," and "tannin" means "crocodile."

But these modern meanings seem far from accurate when related to descriptions given in the Bible text.

Also, these unusually perplexing creatures seem to have stumped the translators of the Bible. English scholars translating the King James Version of the Bible translated "tannin" variously as a whale, serpent, or dragon. "Leviathan" gave them such a great problem that they simply kept the Hebrew noun, giving English another vague word of nebulous definition.

It is certain that the ancient Israelites knew of the Nile crocodile (*Crocodilus niloticus*), and the leviathan we meet in the Book of Job may well be this toothy reptile. Describing the weakness of man compared to this fierce monster, the Bible asks: "Canst thou draw out leviathan with an hook? or his tongue with a cord which thou lettest down? Canst thou put an hook into his nose? or bore his jaw through with a thorn? Will he make many supplications unto thee? will he speak soft words unto thee?" (Job 42:1–3).

The answer to all these questions is a firm no. This leviathan is a very powerful fiend and we are warned: "Lay thine hand upon him, remember the battle, do no more . . . None is so fierce that dare stir him up" (Job 41:8, 10). And Job tells us why leviathan is such an awesome creature, giving a detailed description that seems to define the brutish crocodile: "Who can open the doors of his face? his teeth are terrible round about. His scales are his pride, shut up together as with a close seal. . . . His heart is as firm as a stone; yea, as hard as a piece of the nether millstone. When he raiseth up himself, the mighty are afraid. . . . The sword of him that

lyeth at him cannot hold: the spear, the dart, nor the habergeon. He esteemeth iron as straw, and brass as rotten wood. The arrow cannot make him flee: slingstones are turned with him into stubble. Darts are counted as stubble: he laugheth at the shaking of a spear. Sharp stones are under him: he spreadeth sharp pointed things upon the mire. He maketh the deep to boil like a pot: he maketh the sea like a pot of ointment" (Job 41:14–15, 24–31).

For a few verses, Job's description seems to slip into the realm of myth, or at least extreme exaggeration, giving the leviathan a few incredible characteristics that could not possibly be attributed to any living animal: "By his neesings [sneezings] a light doth shine, and his eyes are like the eyelids of the mornings. Out of his mouth go burning lamps, and sparks of fire leap out. Out of his nostrils goeth smoke, as out of a seething pot or caldron. His breath kindleth coals, and a flame goeth out of his mouth" (Job 41:18–21).

While this last description seems to be more the product of fires of an imagination than an observation of fires sprouting from leviathan, the zoology that precedes it appears to point toward the crocodile: a mouth like a door, containing terrible teeth; a tough, armored skin, plated with close linked scales; a habitat of shallow and rocky mire as well as deeper water which he can thrash to froth.

Surely, it seems most probable that Job was thinking of the crocodile when he wrote "leviathan." But in other passages of Scripture it appears as if the "tannin" is our crocodile.

Ezekiel had unkind words for the Egyptian Pharaoh, likening him to the crocodiles that infest the Nile: "Speak,

and say, Thus saith the Lord God; Behold, I am against thee, Pharaoh king of Egypt, the great dragon [tannin] that lieth in the midst of his rivers, which hath said, My river is mine own, and I have made it for myself" (Ezekiel 29:3). In another passage, tannin is translated as "whale," but the description betrays it to be a crocodile. Addressing the Egyptian Pharaoh, the prophet said, "thou art as a whale [tannin] in the seas: and thou camest forth with thy rivers, and troubledst the waters with thy feet, and fouledst their rivers" (Ezekiel 32:2).

Jeremiah extends the contempt to Israel's oppressors from the Euphrates River: "Nebuchadnezzer the king of Babylon hath devoured me, he hath crushed me, he hath made me an empty vessel, he hath swallowed me up like a dragon [tannin], he hath filled his belly with my delicates, he hath cast me out" (Jeremiah 51:34).

The crocodile was found in Israel until the nineteenth century, inhabiting small rivers and streams along the Mediterranean coast. About thirty miles south of Haifa, there is a small river that still bears the name of its ferocious former inhabitants, Nahal Tanninim (River of Crocodiles). It is presumed by many that the primordial reptile, a living fossil from the age of dinosaurs, came to ancient Israel from Egypt. Perhaps when the Nile was in flood, some of its twenty-foot crocodiles were swept out into the Mediterranean. Or, possibly, they may have left the Nile of their own accord, wandering downstream in search of food until they were carried into the sea by a tide. In either case, the crocodile could survive in salt water for a limited time, long enough to find its way back to freshwater along the Levantine coast.

Sometimes, both leviathan and tannin defy identification with the crocodile. Rather, some sort of serpent, or sea monster, seems to be a more appropriate identification.

In the Creation, we are told: "And God created great whales [tannin]" (Genesis 1:21). The psalmist seems to be alluding to a venomous serpent: "the dragon [tannin] shalt thou trample under feet" (Psalms 91:13). Another psalm alludes to a great sea monster: "So is this great and wide sea, wherein are things creeping innumerable, both small and great beasts. There go the ships: there is that leviathan, whom thou hast made to play therein" (Psalms 104:25–26).

Isaiah draws us yet a different picture. Prophesizing divine judgment of the enemies of Israel, he said: "In that day the Lord with his sore and great and strong sword shall punish leviathan, the piercing serpent, even leviathan that crooked serpent; and he shall slay the dragon [tannin] that is in the sea" (Isaiah 27:1). It seems probable that the two leviathans mentioned are images of Egypt and Assyria while the tannin symbolizes the Philistines. But, zoologically, it is important to remember that Isaiah makes mention of two different leviathans, suggesting that the name may be used in a generic sense, describing various water-dwelling animals.

A careful study of this passage may help us develop some vital clues toward understanding the identity of these great aquatic monsters. First, it seems to be that there are at least two specific sea animals known as leviathan: the "piercing serpent," which implies a beast with a stiff, sharp edge—possibly the crocodile with its piercing teeth—and then there is the "crooked serpent," which may be some sort of giant sea snake, squid, or octopus. The word "leviathan," incidentally, stems from a root meaning "twisted in folds."

These dual identities for leviathan tend to reinforce the theory that the name is a generic identification for various sea monsters. This also seems to be true for tannin, and perhaps both tannin and leviathan may have been interchangeable.

This is suggested in the Psalms: "Thou didst divide the sea by thy strength: thou brakest the heads of the dragons [tannin] in the waters. Thou brakest the heads of leviathan in pieces and gavest him to be meat to the people inhabiting the wilderness" (Psalms 74:13–14).

Whatever the identity of these monstrous beasts, we can be sure that whenever we meet them in the Bible, they are there to symbolize some element of powerful hostility. They are the symbols of power which can only be overcome by divine assistance: "Awake, awake, put on strength, O arm of the Lord; awake, as in the ancient days, in the generations of old. Art thou not it that hath cut Rahab [symbol of the pagan Jericho that fell before Joshua's trumpets], and wounded the dragon [tannin]?" (Isaiah 51:9).

LIONS

"The lion hath roared, who will not fear?"   (AMOS 3:8)

THE LION is courage. It is strength and righteousness, brutality and gentleness. The lion is the lamb. It is the symbol of authority, the instrument of Satan, the image of God.

When a lion (*Panthera leo*) treads through episodes of Scripture, the reader can always be sure the presence of that awesome beast is of central significance. At times, the lion is elevated beyond his normally impressive stature and assumes direct identification with God.

Reverence for the absolute power and authority of God is a prime tenet common to each of the monotheistic religions, and on a symbolic scale, there is no image that can match the lion in compelling profound respect. Direct identification with God is the lion's greatest distinction.

Many of the attributes ascribed to the "king of beasts" serve well to portray related aspects of the Universal King. The roar of the lion is a powerful echo of a commandment of God. "The lion hath roared, who will not fear? the Lord God hath spoken, who can but prophesy?" (Amos 3:8).

Divine ferocity is seen in the lion. A woeful Job, beset by continued misfortunes, turns to God and laments: "Thou huntest me as a fierce lion" (Job 10:16).

Divine authority is seen in the lion. God, angered by the sinfulness of man, forsakes His seclusion "as a lion" to mete justice to the wrongdoers (Jeremiah 25:38).

Such imagery is not restricted to Jewish Scripture. The Koran tells of sinners running from admonishment: "As they were frightened asses, Fleeing from a lion" (Surah 75: Al-Mudath-thir: 51, 52).

Although the lion reaches its highest scriptural stature as

an image of God, its most common use is as a symbol of a servant of God. St. John the Divine, recording a vision of the throne of God, describes a dazzling spectacle of brilliant rainbows arcing over crystalline seas. And immediately before the throne of the Almighty, John describes four beasts: "the first beast was like a lion" (Revelation 4:7), he says, almost as if it were kept as an earthly monarch would keep a pedigree watchdog or pet.

Through the more than one hundred references to lions in Scripture, most of the allusions suggest that the lion is indeed a servant, and perhaps the greatest servant, of God. There is no scriptural record of a lion not fulfilling his ordained role. When God commands, the lion obeys.

During the reign of Jeroboam, a prophet roamed the hills just north of Jerusalem. He had been forbidden by God to accept either bread or water from those he met during his travels. But, in a deception, the prophet broke the divine command. After a simple meal, the prophet continued on his way only to be met and slain by a lion: ". . . therefore the Lord hath delivered him unto the lion, which hath torn him, and slain him, according to the word of the Lord" (I Kings 13:26).

Scriptural lions not only execute on command, but they preserve. A favorite example is the story of Daniel in the lion's den. Persecuted for praying to God, Daniel was thrown into a lion's den by order of the Persian King Darius. A day later, the faithful Daniel emerged unscathed, claiming: "My God hath sent his angel, and hath shut the lions' mouths, that they have not hurt me" (Daniel 6:22).

Isaiah describes the servants of God who will seek vengeance against the unfaithful: ". . . they shall roar like young lions: yea, they shall roar, and lay hold of the prey, and carry it away safe, and none shall deliver it" (Isaiah 5:29).

As the lion is established as a symbolic servant of God, it is also adopted as a symbol of others who stand within the shadow of divine authority. In assigning a fateful image to each of the twelve tribes of Israel, God proclaims, "Judah is a lion's whelp" (Genesis 49:9), and thus seals the destiny of the tribe that is to hold the scepter of leadership. From this point, the "Lion of Judah" will grow to become the king of men, much as its namesake is the king of beasts.

The image is enhanced by subsequent prophesy relating the violent, yet victorious conquests of Canaan: "Behold, the people shall rise up as a great lion, and lift up himself as a young lion: he shall not lie down until he eat of the prey, and drink the blood of the slain" (Numbers 23:24).

As the lion is the symbol of a Jewish state in victory, so it is in defeat. Ezekiel relates the parable of the lion's whelps, an extended metaphor that tells the lamentable history of Jewish captivity in both Egypt and Babylon. The story tells how the King of Babylon captured the Israelite lion, and "they brought him into holds, that his voice should no more be heard upon the mountains of Israel" (Ezekiel 19:9).

The figurative lion, the Jewish state, has survived. Captivity and dispersion did not destroy it, and the state of Israel today flourishes. The literal Judean lion has not found such a favorable fate. The last lion to roam the Judean wilderness disappeared some seven hundred years ago. The last wild lions to inhabit any of the lands of Scripture were driven from the thickets of Mesopotamia, the ancient Babylon, during the nineteenth century. The closest the lion approaches the lands of Scripture today is into parts of Iran and northeast Africa.

But we have enough references to capture a glimpse of the lion's domain during the ancient days of Scripture. There are several references that mention the lion roaming the hills around Jerusalem. And Jeremiah records that the great beast prowled the dense growths of the Jordan valley. During the Assyrian occupation, lions roved the hills of Samaria (II Kings 17:25), and at the time of Solomon, lions were known to range the mountain areas of Amana, Shenir, and Hermon (Song of Songs 4:8).

No longer. The mighty lion is driven from his ancestral lair—but not before he left some lasting images, foremost of which is the manifestation of courage.

The lion is courage, and not merely the simple definition of courage. Scriptural courage is a much more abstract virtue than simple boldness. Rather, in Scripture, courage is normally of divine inspiration and connotes a certain amount of godly assistance and righteousness. We find this connection in passages such as "the righteous are bold as a lion" (Proverbs 28:1).

The young David, who slew lions as a shepherd boy, exemplified the scriptural concept of courage when he met the mighty Goliath. David cried to the Philistine: "Thou comest to me with a sword, and with a spear, and with a shield: but I come to thee in the name of the Lord of hosts, the God of the armies of Israel, whom thou hast defied" (I Samuel 17:45). And that was all David needed to ensure victory.

Christian Scripture treats the lion with seeming paradox. As we have seen, St. John envisioned a lion directly before the throne of God, closer than any man or angel dared to approach, a position of high esteem. But the apostle Paul uses the lion as the image of terrible oppression in pagan Rome. Writing to Timothy during his second ordeal before Emperor Nero, Paul says, "and I was delivered out of the mouth of the lion" (II Timothy 4:17). And the apostle Peter used the lion as an image of even greater evil, advising his readers: "Be sober, be vigilant; because your adversary the devil, as a roaring lion, walketh about, seeking whom he may devour" (I Peter 5:8).

In a stark turnabout, John elevates the lion to identification with Christ at the Day of Judgment. The setting is dramatic. The great book, which is to reveal the coming Kingdom of Heaven, sits unopened, its secrets locked behind seven seals: "And one of the elders saith unto me, Weep not: behold, the Lion of the tribe of Judah, the Root of David, hath prevailed to open the book, and to loose the seven seals thereof" (Revelation 5:5).

The lion and the root are one—Christ—claiming both blood lineage and prophetic authority. He appears as the Lamb, opening the book, thereby reestablishing the lion-lamb paradox.

This paradox echoes back to earlier days of Scripture, to one of the most beautiful prophesies recorded by man. It is Isaiah's prophesy of the peaceable kingdom: "and the calf and the young lion and the fatling [shall dwell] together" (Isaiah 11:6). Not only will the lion dwell with the lamb, but it will learn to scorn violence and adopt the more passive ways of the gentler animals: "and the lion shall eat straw like the ox" (Isaiah 11:7).

ORYXES (UNICORNS)

". . . he hath as it were the strength of an unicorn" (NUMBERS 24:8)

WHEN A WONDER of Creation is touched by the imagination of a human mind, the distinction between truth and fiction becomes elusive.

For example, the fabulous unicorn, which parades as the image of unbridled strength through many episodes in the King James Version of the Bible, appears to be only a myth. But a little research and some common sense may combine to suggest that the myth of the unicorn, like most other myths, has a basis in fact.

The ancient Hebrew writers of the Old Testament called the animal *re'em*, a name that today is usually interpreted as a wild ox. But during the past four thousand years, myths have been born and real animals have passed into extinction, leaving us with some complicated and vague possibilities to unravel.

Using the Bible as a prime source, we may get a rough idea of what kind of animal the unicorn, or *re'em*, was. The strength of the unicorn has been known since the times of the Patriarchs. Describing Jacob leading the Israelites into the land of Canaan, the Bible says, "God brought him forth out of Egypt; he hath as it were the strength of an unicorn: he shall eat up the nations his enemies, and shall break their bones, and pierce them through with his arrows" (Numbers 24:8).

The strength of the unicorn is again mentioned when Moses blessed the tribes. Turning to Joseph, Moses said, "his horns are like the horns of unicorns: with them he shall push the people together to the ends of the earth: and they are the ten thousands of Ephraim, and they are the thousands of Manasseh" (Deuteronomy 33:17).

While the unicorn is the symbol of extraordinary strength, it is also a strength that cannot be tamed. Job tells of

the unicorn's refusal to submit to the yoke of domestication, suggesting that such unbridled power is untrustworthy: "Will the unicorn be willing to serve thee, or abide by thy crib? Canst thou bind the unicorn with his band into the furrow? or will he harrow the valleys after thee? Wilt thou trust him, because his strength is great? or wilt thou leave thy labour to him? Wilt thou believe him, that he will bring home thy seed, and gather it into thy barn?" (Job 39:9–12).

We find also that the animal's horn is an item of particular biblical interest. It sounds as a unique trumpet of glory and praise. David, in a moving prayer, beseeches God to hear him: "for thou hast heard me from the horns of the unicorns" (Psalms 22:21). Again, the trumpet of the unicorn's horn is heard in a Sabbath song: "But my horn shalt thou exalt like the horn of an unicorn: I shall be anointed with fresh oil" (Psalms 92:10).

The unicorn is unbridled strength; its horn trumpets glorious praise. Although the animal might be used for agricultural work, it refuses domestication. Working with this evidence, and ignoring all the unicorn stories that have developed in later years, it seems most probable that the *re'em* was some sort of wild bovine.

Many scholars believe the *re'em* intended by the writers of Scripture was the now-extinct aurochs (*Bos primigenisus*), a brawny wild ox that once inhabited much of the Eurasian landmass, including the lands of Scripture. This theory is supported by the ancient Assyrian language, a Semitic tongue related to Hebrew, in which *rimu* was the word used to identify the aurochs.

Although some scholars suggest other possibilities, including the unwieldy rhinoceros and the subarctic reindeer, the probability of these ideas appears rather remote. At present, it seems that the aurochs, which is considered by many to be the ancestor of modern cattle, is our *re'em*. The species has been extinct since the seventeenth century.

But the aurochs simply doesn't fit our modern image of the unicorn. It lacked the grace, speed, and unique single horn of the animal modern man knows as the unicorn.

A likely explanation may be found in some faulty information fed to the Bible translators commissioned by King James back in 1611 C.E. This information came from the English Crusaders who, during their adventures in the Holy Land, may have seen a few Arabian oryx (*Oryx leucoryx*) from a distance. The Arabian oryx, now a rare and endangered species, is a type of desert antelope that is almost entirely white. It has two long and almost straight horns that, when viewed from a profile, appear as one.

The Arabian oryx is a shy creature with very keen eyesight. When in danger, it flees at a gallop. It is quite unlikely that any Crusader riding a heavily armored charger could ever approach much closer than a few hundred yards before the swift oryx would disappear into the desert's dust.

Historic records indicate that the Crusaders had a tendency to exaggerate their stories after their return to Europe. Minor encounters became great battles, a tiny wood lot became a great forest, and perhaps the timid Arabian oryx became a fierce unicorn. Stories of the fabulous unicorn spread across Europe, and evidence of its popularity can be seen today in medieval folklore, tapestry, woodcuts, and the 1611 English translation of the Bible.

Today, not one Arabian oryx survives in the wild. The last one was killed a few years ago by hunters in the desert sultanate of Oman.

Fortunately, there is a small ray of hope. In 1963 the Fauna Preservation Society conducted "Operation Oryx," the first attempt to build a captive breeding herd of seriously endangered species. Working at the Maytag Zoo in Phoenix, Arizona, the program collected four oryx and nurtured them into a growing herd that held the species back from the brink of extinction.

Then, in May of 1978 the Hai Bar Society, an Israeli conservation group, and the Holy Land Conservation Fund, an American conservation group, organized a project that would return the Arabian oryx to its ancestral habitat. Four pairs of the species were purchased from the Los Angeles Zoo and were shipped to Israel, where they are carefully protected in a special reserve area located in the Negev Desert. In the fall of 1978, the first fruit of this project was born. The young oryx is the first of its kind to have been born in the Holy Land in perhaps eight centuries. A percentage of the royalties from this book is being used to provide all necessary care for the growth and welfare of this young oryx.

As these animals multiply, and the breeding stock becomes reliable, portions of the herd will be reintroduced back into the wild. If the project proves successful, man may again see the magnificent Arabian oryx galloping across the desert sands of the Middle East.

An interesting sidelight to the rescue of the Arabian oryx is that the effort was also responsible for saving the scimitar-horned oryx, a closely related species. When it appeared that the Arabian oryx was slipping into extinction, and it became impossible to obtain any members of the species to build a breeding herd, the Hai Bar Society and the Holy Land Conservation Fund turned to the scimitar-horned oryx in an attempt to rescue the Arabian's closest living relative. They adopted a plan to form a small breeding herd from the remnants of the few left in the wild, inhabiting the southern fringe of the Sahara.

The plan worked, and a healthy herd now inhabits a reserve area in the Negev. The fortune of this event has just recently become apparent. The long years of drought in the southern Sahara were particularly severe for wildlife that had to compete with domestic herds of cattle and goats for the scant grasses left in the area. When famine set in, the last of these oryx became meals for hungry people.

It is believed that the last scimitar-horned oryx may have vanished from the wild during the past two years. The small herd maintained in the Negev is believed to be one of the species' greatest hope for survival.

OSTRICHES

". . . cruel, like the ostriches in the wilderness" (LAMENTATIONS 4:3)

CRUEL, unclean, mournful, forgetful, stupid, and the inheritor of pagan ruins, the ostrich suffers one of the most reprehensible images in the Holy Scriptures. Even the name that the ancient Hebrews gave this ill-favored bird, *ya'en,* means "greedy."

However, it appears that all this derision is not entirely justified. For the most part, the ancient writers of the Bible drew some pretty faulty conclusions from what were essentially good observations. And this is at least partly understandable, since this gigantic, flightless bird is quite unlike any other animal.

For example, Job, whose precise observations of nature give him fine credentials for commenting on this unusual species, noted: "Gavest thou . . . wings and feathers unto the ostrich? Which leaveth her eggs in the earth, and warmeth

them in dust, And forgetteth that the foot may crush them, or that the wild beast may break them. She is hardened against her young ones, as though they were not hers: her labour is in vain without fear; Because God hath deprived her of wisdom, neither hath he imparted to her understanding. What time she lifteth up herself on high, she scorneth the horse and his rider" (Job 39:13–18).

A modern ornithologist may perhaps suggest that Job was the one lacking in wisdom and understanding, for the ostrich is well suited to its habitat.

In this passage, Job was concerned with the concept of imperfection. Unfortunately, he used the ostrich as his symbol. There are few creatures that fit into their environment more perfectly than the ostrich.

The whole Book of Job recognizes the symbiotic relations

of all creatures. No species is perfect enough to survive alone, but the imperfections of each are balanced by the creative hand of God, giving a perfection to the universe.

Although Job's religious message carries a theological validity, his zoological conclusions seem inadequate. The ostrich may surely have some imperfections, but they are not the ones mentioned by Job. For example, the prophet is contemptuous of the ostrich because it nests on the ground. But then, there simply aren't any other places for a three-hundred-pound bird to keep its eggs in the middle of a barren desert.

The ostrich is, however, well adapted to this arid and demanding habitat. Its three-pound eggs are ochre-colored, blending well with the dust and sand. And their tough shells are extremely difficult to break. When its nest is threatened, the ostrich has a reputation for putting up a terribly vigorous defense. Marauders are first greeted by a flourish of hissing, grunting, and generally hostile wing beating. When quarters close, an attacker may be surprised to learn that ostriches, like other birds, stand on legs that have the capability of kicking forward. Their knees bend in the opposite direction of most other animals, and can deliver an accurate and powerful kick to almost any predator foolish enough to risk a frontal attack.

When Job observed the ostrich "leaveth her eggs," he was probably watching either very young adults or mature adults at dusk. Young adult ostriches seem to have difficulty nesting on their first eggs. They seem to mature biologically before they mature behaviorally. Thus, there is sometimes a period when an ostrich may be laying eggs, but apparently tends to ignore them. After a few months, however, the ostrich's behavior catches up, and both parents get down to the serious demands of nesting. From this point on, ostriches make the most devoted and protective parents.

It's also possible that Job was watching the mature ostriches at dusk. Through the day, the female ostrich patiently hovers over her eggs, shielding them from the blistering desert sun while at the same time absorbing the fullest strength of the solar burden on her own back. At dusk, she rises and lets the cooling breeze waft over them. For a while, the eggs remain uncovered, but as the chilling night sets in, the male takes his turn, keeping the eggs warm until dawn when the female returns to bear the heat of the new day.

Job is particularly accurate at one point; the ostrich is truly capable of scorning a horse and rider. The swiftest of all cursorial birds, the ostrich can jog along at thirty miles an hour over loose desert sands, and that's about as fast as most thoroughbred race horses can run on a firm, manicured track.

Labeled "unclean" by the laws of kosher, the ostrich was occasionally used as the image of moral uncleanliness. In Jeremiah's lament over the infidelity of Israel, he said: "the daughter of my people is become cruel, like the ostriches in the wilderness" (Lamentations 4:3). Job, mourning his own fall from esteem, cried: "I am . . . a companion of ostriches" (Job 30:29). In both cases, the writers obviously were familiar with the jostling and disconcert that normally accompany a flock of ostriches. But this is the maintenance of the "pecking order," a trait common among almost all birds right down to the barnyard chicken. It only appears more severe when the birds are eight feel tall and weigh twice as much as most men.

Isaiah, noting the ostrich's preference for the most desolate quarters of the desert, uses the great bird as a fitting symbol of desolation that is to overtake the corruptions of pagan Babylon: "But wild beasts of the desert will lie down there, and its [Babylon's] houses will be full of howling creatures; there ostriches will dwell" (Isaiah 34:13).

A raging Micah takes this same symbol of an ostrich standing over desolation and bends it back to point out the corruptions in himself and his own people. Prophesizing the vengeance of God in dealing with the unfaithful, Micah said: "I will go stripped and naked; I will make lamentation like the jackals, and mourning like the ostriches" (Micah 1:8).

The ostrich has had to deal with more than a bad image. Although observant Jews would refuse an ostrich stew, other less discerning people have been known to hunt ostrich for its meat. Still others hunted the bird for its rich plumage, which was popular on women's finery until earlier in this century. Good eyesight and a fast running speed were enough to save the big bird until the invention of the high-powered rifle and automobile.

The Syrian ostrich (*Struthio camelus syriacus*), observed by Job, Jeremiah, Isaiah, and other writers of Scripture, is today extinct. Modern weapons exterminated one of the living links to the origins of Western monotheistic religion. The last known Syrian ostrich was killed and eaten in the Arabian desert during World War II.

Currently, a close relative of the extinct bird of Scripture is being introduced into Israel's Negev Desert under protected status. The Ethiopian ostrich (*Struthio camelus ethiopus*) is expected to thrive in the Middle Eastern desert home in the coming years.

Incidentally, there are no scriptural passages that allude to the ostrich's reputation for burying its head in the sand when faced with danger. And this is fortunate, because the reputation is not based on fact. However, when danger does approach, the ostrich does something that probably gave rise to the myth. Threatened from a distance, the ostrich flattens itself on the ground and presses its long neck to the earth, closing its eyes to a mere squint. Its camouflaged color and low profile make the big bird very difficult to see, and even seasoned hunters have admitted losing an ostrich to its camouflaged escape.

If danger approaches too closely, the ostrich can quickly spring to its feet and try to make a successful escape by running hard over the most difficult terrain in the area.

While Scripture seems to have relegated the ostrich to a contemptible image, the ostrich egg is highly prized. Christian traditions include an ostrich egg motif pendant suspended beneath a lamp, a symbol that suggests Jesus watching over the Christian Church with the vigilance of an ostrich guarding its eggs.

In Islam the ostrich egg is considered an object of great beauty. The Koran describes the enlightened expressions of those who have surrendered themselves to the will of Allah as "those of modest gaze, with lovely eyes, pure as they were hidden ostrich eggs" (Surah 37: As-Saffat:48–49).

PYGARGS (ADDAXES)

"These are the beasts which ye shall eat . . . the pygarg" (DEUTERONOMY 14:4, 5)

WHAT'S a pygarg? What manner of beast is it?

Mentioned only once in Scripture, the pygarg is a difficult animal to identify. We have no physical descriptions of this animal, nor is it ever used as a symbol for a particular trait that may give us a hint to its identity. We start this inquiry with few clues, but enough, perhaps, to speculate and even establish a tentative identity.

First, we have the name given this animal in the King James Version of the Bible. It's called "pygarg" from the Greek *pygargos*, which means "white-rumped." Turning to the original Hebrew text, we find this animal identified as *dishon*, a noun stemming from a verb that means "to leap."

Next, we observe its scriptural context. Listed in a catalog of "clean" or "kosher" wild animals, we may assume that the pygarg is also of this nature. It most probably conforms to the requirements of kosher law by having a split hoof and ruminant digestion.

Combining this evidence, we may hypothesize that the pygarg, or dishon, is a mammal, standing on four legs, and it may have some distinctive white markings. Its hooves are split, it chews the cud, it is relatively agile, and it is indigenous to the Middle East. Also, since it is mentioned only once in Scripture, we may assume that it is a relatively uncommon animal, and probably inhabits areas a good distance from human communities and cultivated farms.

Now, another clue may be obtained through the etymology of tribal names in the Middle East. The ancients of the area had a habit of identifying a good many of their tribes with particular animals common to tribal lands. Thus, in the Book of Genesis, we find ancient Hebrew tribes, such as Naphtali,

likened to the deer that wandered the tribe's Galilean home-land. Issachar was likened to the domestic ass that became such a common beast of burden in the fertile valley of Jezreel, where Issachar made its home.

The use of animal identification was not restricted to the Hebrew tribes, but was relatively common with all the ancient people of the area. Thus, we find other Middle Eastern tribes bearing animal names: the tribe of Asad (lion) and the tribe of Kuraysh (shark) are two early Arabic examples.

There was also a tribe of Dishon. In the Bible, the Dishon were ". . . the dukes of the Horites, the children of Seir in the land of Edom" (Genesis 36:21). The Horites were primitive cave dwellers in the barren Edomite wasteland, southeast of the Dead Sea. The tribal patriarch's name, Seir, means "rough and hairy." If the animal dishon of Deuteron-omy is linked with the tribe of the same name, we may assume that it must be a hardy desert animal, capable of surviving in the onerous wastelands of Edom that stretch eastward from the burning Negev Desert.

With the clues we have assembled thus far, there are several animals that would fit the requirements of the pygarg. So now we must eliminate a few, narrowing the field. First, we can eliminate the Revised Standard Bible's translation of "dishon" as an ibex. The ancient Hebrews had a different name for this beautiful cousin of the common goat and called it *ye'el*, a name that appears in several passages of the Bible and is generally considered to be accepted.

For the same reason, we can eliminate the gazelle, which elsewhere is well known as *zvi*. Some scholars suggest the Arabian oryx is the pygarg, particularly since its ancient Akkadian name, *da'assu*, seems to have a close linguistic link to the Hebrew *dishon*. But then, the oryx seems to fit more neatly into identification with the Hebrew *teo*, the unicorn of the King James Version.

There is another animal that roamed the Middle Eastern deserts that has not yet been identified here. It is the addax (*Addax nasomaculata*), an antelope that well fits all the requirements that have been set for the pygarg.

This large and picturesque animal is a true denizen of the desert, capable of surviving the most intense climate and terrain of the Middle East. In fact, the British naturalist H. B. Tristram, making a survey of Palestine a century ago, reported the addax as "a scarce and very large Antelope," which lived to the south and east of Palestine—exactly where the biblical Edom was located, the homeland of the tribe of Dishon.

A beautiful animal, the addax carries gracefully spiraling horns that twist more than a yard above its head. Its coat is a gray-brown, except for a broad swath of white on its rear and underparts; a fine animal to be identified with the Greek *pygargos*.

Powerful legs and broad hooves make the addax a relatively fleet animal for crossing loose desert sands, and perhaps this characteristic is the root for its Hebrew name. Few other animals can leap across soft sands with the facility of the addax.

Another remarkable characteristic of the addax is its ability to survive in the desert indefinitely without drinking water. Naturalists generally agree that the addax gets enough moisture by grazing on the sparse hygroscopic vegetation of the desert, particularly in the early morning when it is moist with dew.

The addax was rare in ancient times, but it was definitely known. Paintings inside Egyptian tombs from 4,500 years ago show addax captured and tethered to stakes. This was done at just about the same time the ancient Hebrew tribes were being held in Egyptian bondage. Thus, it seems sure that the ancient Hebrews must have known of the addax, and presumably had a name for it. Since no other biblical name seems to fit, and "dishon" seems to fit well, it may be a reasonable conclusion to consider the addax as our animal here.

Although the addax was uncommon even in biblical days, it is even more so today. Last seen in biblical lands about a century ago, when Tristram made his survey, the addax has been forced back into the most remote depths of the desert.

While the addax is extremely wary, and flees at the least provocation, it is no match for the mechanized hunter. Scattered across North Africa during the beginning of the twentieth century, the addax was frequently hunted by Italian troops during the 1930s. This hunting, combined with hunts organized at North African oil drilling sites, have pressed the addax even deeper into the Sahara. The last herds surviving in the wild today are restricted to a small area in the desert areas of Mali, several hundred miles north of Timbuktu. And even these herds have been severely decimated in recent years because of the great drought in the area.

One note of hope, however, lies in a special program being conducted by the Israeli Nature Reserves Authority at its Hai Bar sanctuary in the Negev. The Authority has purchased several addax that it had located in various zoos around the world, forming them into a small breeding herd. The herd produced its first newborn addax in 1972, the first addax to be born in the shadow of the Edomite mountains in more than a century. As the breeding herd develops in numbers, the Authority plans on releasing small groups of addax back into the wild, back into the land they roamed a century ago, back into the land they roamed forty-five centuries ago.

RAVENS

". . . and I have commanded the ravens to feed thee there" (1 KINGS 17:4)

THE HARSH CAW OF the raven is a voice from a dangerous wilderness. It is a frightful song of evil omen and terrifying prophesy. The raven's rasping cry, its somber plumage, and its carrion diet together cast a decidedly unwholesome and macabre image.

Yet, for all the rancor heaped against this gregarious bird, the raven also possesses a certain beauty, both in appearance and in temperament. The raven's lustrous, even radiantly mysterious ebony feathers become an image of sensuous beauty in the Song of Songs: "his locks are . . . black as a raven" (Song of Songs 5:11).

But it is the raven's rebellious temperament that gives it a beauty of a deeper sense. It is an intellectual beauty that has proliferated from Holy Scripture through all the literatures of monotheistic cultures. It is the raven's jealously guarded independence within a generally predictable character, its vivacity, and its role as a constant antagonist cast as a rebel.

The raven was the first animal to inhabit the postdiluvian world. When Noah's ark touched ground on the slopes of Mount Ararat, he threw open a window to see the new world purged of its wickedness. Then: "he sent forth a raven, which went forth to and fro, until the waters were dried up from off the earth" (Genesis 8:7).

But the raven flew away, never to return. It left behind only a sinister prophesy. It is a natural survivor and an omen of evil that will be with the world through every catastrophe until the end of time. If repeated cataclysms purge the world of wickedness, there will always be a surviving raven, waiting in the shadows to return to the world after each destruction as a harbinger of new wickedness.

The Bible prophesizes that a vengeful God will again destroy a wicked world. This time, it will be a conflagration of burning pitch, brimstone, and smoke. But even this disaster will not be the ultimate devastation. The world will continue, the prophet tells us, "and the raven shall dwell in it" (Isaiah 34:11).

The Koran adds a footnote to the story of Noah, and tells why the raven, set loose after the Flood, never returned to the ark. It had found the carcass of an animal killed by the Deluge, a symbol of the wickedness that had been swept from the face of the earth. But the raven started to feed on the carcass, taking into its body the fiber of wickedness, the germ for renewed wickedness.

Because of the raven's unreliability, Noah then chose a dove to scout out the reborn world. The dove proved more dependable and, after flying about for a while, returned with a twig from an olive tree to prove the earth could again sustain life.

But, in Scripture, sometimes the raven is assigned a critical role, and these tasks it performs with efficient thoroughness. It might have ignored the hopes of Noah, but when commanded by God, the raven is absolutely faithful.

Occasionally, the divinely appointed task is rather noble, such as when God commanded the ravens to feed the prophet Elijah in his refuge by the brook of Cherith: "and the ravens brought him bread and flesh in the morning, and bread and flesh in the evening" (I Kings 17:6).

Other tasks are less humanitarian, but the raven performs what is commanded with the ruthlessness of a military shock force: "The eye that mocketh at his father, and despiseth to obey his mother, the ravens of the valley shall pick it out" (Proverbs 30:17).

The Koran narrates another lamentable task ordered of the raven: teaching man to bury his brother: "Then Allah sent a raven scratching up the ground, to show him [Cain] how to hide his brother's naked corpse. He said: Woe unto me! Am I not able to be as this raven and not hide my brother's corpse? And he became repentant" (Surah 5: Al Ma'idah:31).

Whether the raven is assigned to missions of compassion, justice, or destruction, it will forever be one of God's protected species. The psalmist, praising the generosity of God, observed, "He giveth to the beast his food, and to the young ravens which cry" (Psalms 147:9). Although the raven is promised the requirements of life, it is also doomed to a life of scorn. It is an unclean bird, and "every raven after his kind" (Leviticus 11:15) is an abomination.

The Hebrew word for raven is *orev*, which also denotes the whole order of Corvidae, lumping ravens, crows, jackdaws, and other related birds into a single identification. The name *orev* seems particularly close to *erev*, Hebrew for "evening," suggesting the raven may be named for the darker hours.

The uncleanness of the raven, or more common to English-speaking people its close cousin the crow, has become part of our idiomatic speech. When someone is said to "eat crow" we suggest that they are submitting to great humiliation; they are forced to swallow something that is entirely disagreeable.

The Arab world knows the raven as *ghurab*, or more

familiarly as *ghurah al-baya*—the carrion crow. For Bedouin Moslems, this bird is a symbol of sadness in separation. Desert folklore attributes this image to the raven's habit of descending on camps as they are abandoned to pick through what scraps might be scavenged. A traveler who reaches a camp inhabited by ravens knows he has missed his connection, the tribe has moved on without him. Hence, the sight of ravens at the campsite means sadness.

Some superstitious Bedouin find great security with the raven. A raven's beak, carried as a talisman, is said to ward off bad luck better than any Westerner's rabbit's foot. And dried raven's blood is considered an invaluable elixir in the treatment of hemorrhoids.

The order of Corvidae has spread around the world and is common in each continent. There are several species found in biblical lands, particularly the brown-necked raven, which is found in many desert areas, including the barren hills around Jerusalem.

SCORPIONS

". . . as the scorpions of the earth have power" (REVELATION 9:3)

COMMISSIONING Ezekiel as a prophet among the Israelites captive in Babylon, God warned him of frightful days ahead: "And thou, son of man, be not afraid of them, neither be afraid of their words, though briers and thorns be with thee, and thou dost dwell among scorpions" (Ezekiel 2:6).

Here, as elsewhere in Scripture, the scorpion symbolizes a terribly hostile environment. And this symbol is well chosen, for the scorpion is a terribly hostile creature.

A venomous arachnid, related to spiders, the scorpion is the image of evil and often symbolizes a devil incarnate who can only be overcome by people on a divine mission or with divine protection, as Ezekiel.

When Jesus commissioned seventy disciples on a mission to preach the Christian gospel, he used the scorpion as an image of danger that he promised protection against: "Behold, I give unto you power to tread on serpents and scorpions, and over all the power of the enemy: and nothing shall by any means hurt you" (Luke 10:19).

As the Israelites prepared to cross the Jordan River into their Promised Land, they were warned not to relax too much in the luxury of the land of milk and honey. They were warned not to feel too secure in their new community and forget their God: "Who led thee through that great and terrible wilderness, wherein were fiery serpents, and scorpions, and drought" (Deuteronomy 8:15).

In each of these cases, as elsewhere in Scripture, the scorpion is an insidious image which is held at bay only by the beneficence of an omnipotent God.

The reason why the scorpion is considered such an

abominable creature may lie in its anatomical character and symbiosis. In many respects, the scorpion lives in a realm often considered evil. A nocturnal hunter, the scorpion normally seeks its prey under cover of night and spends daylight hours hidden like Dracula in the tomb, squeezing into darkened burrows and crevices. The scorpion can tolerate desert heat likened to the fires of hell. It is a solitary creature, shunning society for a more reclusive life.

Symbiotically, the scorpion likes to live in or near human communities. Especially in the desert, where nighttime temperatures frequently plummet to a frosty chill, the lethal scorpion seeks the warmth of the human community.

For centuries, soldiers who have bivouacked in the tropics quickly learned to carefully shake and inspect their boots before putting them on in the morning. The warm leather cocoon is a favorite haunt of marauding scorpions, and scorpion stings suffered by uncautious soldiers have long been major hazards for troops on the campaign.

The most virulent characteristic of the scorpion is its five-segmented, venomous tail. This tail (actually part of the abdomen) was known and respected for its power all through the days of Scripture. St. John the Divine described the painful weapon: "And they had tails like unto scorpions, and there were stings in their tails" (Revelation 9:10).

The poison in the scorpion's stinger is a weapon that is rarely respected enough. While most people will make a special effort to avoid a poisonous snake, scorpions, perhaps because of their small size, simply don't get this kind of respect.

But the simple fact is that some varieties of scorpions have venom potent enough to kill an adult male in the best of health. Even the sting of the least poisonous scorpion causes severe pain and a long, tormenting illness. Indeed, even in the United States, where we have plenty of rattlesnakes, cottonmouths, copperheads, and even a few poisonous coral snakes, more people are killed by scorpions every year than by all species of snakes combined. The same goes for Mexico, where there are an even greater variety of poisonous snakes.

The pincers, or more properly "pedipalpi," that are carried menacingly in front of the scorpion are essentially harmless.

St. John, describing the great cataclysm of doomsday, gave creatures climbing from the bottomless pit the strength of scorpions, to seek and sting all those who did not bear the seal of God upon their foreheads: "And to them it was given that they should not kill them, but that they should be tormented five months: and their torment was as the torment of a scorpion, when he striketh a man" (Revelation 9:5).

So brutal and burning is the sting of the scorpion that its name was adopted as a nickname for one of the most painful weapons of biblical times. King Rehoboam, refusing to be reconciled with the rebel Jeroboam after he broke the northern portion of Solomon's kingdom away, warned: "my father [Solomon] also chastised you with whips, but I will chastise you with scorpions" (I Kings 12:14). The "scorpion" Rehoboam promised to use is a type of whip with barbed metal tips sewn into it. These tips are sharpened and can be dipped in poison to produce an effect not unlike the sting of a scorpion.

In Hebrew the scorpion is known as *akrav*, stemming from a phrase meaning "to wound the heel." Many species of scorpion are known in the Middle East, and two varieties, the black *Buthus judaicus*, and the yellow *Buthus questriatus*, are the most common. Scorpions can be found almost anywhere in the Holy Land, from back alleys of Jerusalem to the rugged wastes of Sinai. The more poisonous varieties, luckily, seem to prefer the Sinai.

SERPENTS (SNAKES)

". . . that old serpent, called the Devil" (REVELATION 12:9)

THE SERPENT is evil, a malignant fiend eternally plotting mischief and calamity. Cursed by God as the source of human misery, the serpent accomplished its first evil deed at the dawn of human history when only two people, Adam and Eve, inhabited the earth. From this point on, the serpent sustains a wholly disreputable image throughout the rest of Scripture.

It was the serpent that tempted Eve, bringing her to eat from the Tree of Knowledge in the Garden of Eden, and thus bringing about the fall of humanity. Since the serpent acted as a catalyst of events to destroy the paradisiacal creation, God cursed the serpent, relegating it to the position of lowest and most despised beast: "And the Lord God said unto the serpent, Because thou hast done this, thou art cursed above all cattle, and above every beast of the field; upon thy belly shalt

thou go, and dust shalt thou eat all the days of thy life" (Genesis 3:14).

And because the serpent tempted, and humanity assented, God deigned eternal antagonism between them: "And I will put enmity between thee [the serpent] and the woman, and between thy seed and her seed; it shall bruise thy head, and thou shalt bruise his heel" (Genesis 3:15).

Through Scripture, this enmity persists relentlessly. The conflict between man and snake stands as a metaphor of the conflict between understanding and evil. Man, with his ill-gotten faculty of knowledge, is forever at odds with evil. It is a conflict for all time, with knowledge sometimes thwarted by evil and sometimes overcoming it; but never is one side totally victorious.

The evil threat symbolized by the serpent is a theme

found in both Judaic and Christian Scripture. David, lamenting the evilness of men preparing for war, compared them to serpents: "They have sharpened their tongue like a serpent; adders' poison is under their lips" (Psalms 140:3). The apostle Paul, defending his ministry, exhorted the Christian converts of Corinth to beware of subterfuge: "But I fear, lest by any means, as the serpent beguiled Eve through his subtilty, so your minds should be corrupted from the simplicity that is in Christ" (II Corinthians 11:3).

In several instances, there is divine protection from the innate evil of the serpent. God gave Moses the power to control the serpent: "And the Lord said unto him, What is that in thine hand? And he said, A rod. And he said, Cast it on the ground. And he cast it on the ground, and it became a serpent; and Moses fled from before it. And the Lord said unto Moses, Put forth thine hand, and take it by the tail. And he put forth his hand, and caught it, and it became a rod in his hand: That they may believe that the Lord God of their fathers, the God of Abraham, the God of Isaac, and the God of Jacob, hath appeared unto thee" (Exodus 4:2-5). Thus, the serpent-staff of Moses became a symbol of his divine appointment and strength over the forces of evil.

In Christian Scripture, Jesus promised protection to his disciples to the extent that "They shall take up serpents" (Mark 16:18). The disciples preached in an evil and hostile environment, and at least on one occasion, this hostility was quite literally manifest in the serpent. Paul, a prisoner of the Romans, was shipwrecked on the island of Malta. Well received by the natives, the apostle joined them in building a fire: "And when Paul had gathered a bundle of sticks, and laid them on the fire, there came a viper out of the heat, and fastened on his hand" (Acts 28:3). The startled natives expected the poisonous bite to be fatal, but when Paul threw the snake back into the fire without the least harm to himself, they were convinced that he had divine protection.

Of the several species of snakes that inhabit biblical lands, four are venomous: three vipers and one cobra. It is these snakes that count for all the serpent images of evil in Scripture.

The Egyptian cobra (*Naja haje*), known in Hebrew as *peten*, ranges from North Africa into Sinai and the southern Negev. It is easily recognized in Scripture because of its connection with the ancient craft of snake charming. It is obviously the Egyptian cobra referred to in the passage: "Their poison is like the poison of a serpent: they are like the deaf adder that stoppeth her ear; Which will not hearken to the voice of charmers, charming never so wisely" (Psalms 58:4-5). Again, the great beguiler defies beguilement: "For, behold, I will send serpents, cockatrices, among you, which will not be charmed, and they shall bite you, saith the Lord" (Jeremiah 8:17).

Job mentions the Egyptian cobra, also known as the asp, along with the carpet viper (*Echis carinatus*), or Hebrew *efeh*, in his description of the hypocrite: "He shall suck the poison of asps [*peten*]: the viper's [*efeh*] tongue shall slay him" (Job 20:16).

The carpet viper, a highly poisonous snake, is mentioned by Isaiah as living in the southern desert areas of biblical lands, as it does to this day.

The horned viper (*Cerastes cornutus*) is also a denizen of the southern desert areas, and is best known for its ability to bury itself, coiled into loose sand. This ability makes the snake, known in Hebrew as *shefifon*, particularly dangerous, since it strikes from concealment without warning. A horned viper so buried is nearly invisible, since only its eyes protrude above the sand. Frequently, these eyes are mistaken for insects, and unwary birds descend on them with the thought of a quick meal. Instead, the birds find themselves the meal of a deceptive snake.

The tribe of Dan is compared to this hidden viper by the patriarch Jacob: "Dan shall be a serpent [*shefifon*] by the way, an adder in the path" (Genesis 49:17).

The only poisonous snake found normally in the densely populated and cultivated lands of the Middle East is the Palestinian viper (*Vipera palaestina*), called *tsefa* in Hebrew. The Palestinian viper is unique in that it lays eggs, while other vipers give birth to live young. This characteristic was noticed by Isaiah, who also observed that these eggs are poisonous: "They hatch cockatrice' [*tsefa*] eggs . . . he that eateth of their eggs dieth, and that which is crushed breaketh out into a viper" (Isaiah 59:5).

Solomon, warning his son to avoid strange women, compared them to the Palestinian viper: "At the last it biteth like a serpent, and stingeth like an adder [*tsefa*]" (Proverbs 23:32).

While the snake is always a symbol of evil, it is also a creation of God, and has its place in the divine scheme. When the Hebrew tribes complained against God and Moses as they wandered without food or water in the desert, God sent serpents against them as punishment for their rebellious attitude: "And the Lord sent fiery serpents among the people, and they bit the people; and much people of Israel died" (Numbers 21:6).

When the people repented, "the Lord said unto Moses, Make thee a fiery serpent [of brass], and set it upon a pole: and it shall come to pass, that every one that is bitten, when he looketh upon it, shall live" (Numbers 21:8).

There is a hint here of the medicinal healing powers originally attributed to snakes in Egypt, the land the Hebrews had just abandoned. In any event, it appears as if the Hebrews kept the brass serpent long after they had left the desert, and long after its divine healing powers had been taken from it. Centuries later, King Hezekiah rooted out the recidivistic tendencies of the Israelite community, including the destruction of the brass snake that some people had honored in idolatrous worship: "He . . . brake in pieces the brasen serpent that Moses had made: for unto those days the children of Israel did burn incense to it: and he called it Nehushtan" (II Kings 18:4).

Driving out the serpent is the driving out of evil. So it was for Hezekiah and Paul, and so it was with the battle of the angels: "And the great dragon was cast out, that old serpent, called the Devil, and Satan, which deceiveth the whole world" (Revelation 12:9).

SHEEP

"Feed my lambs" (JOHN 21:15)

THE ESSENTIAL MEANING OF all Scripture is contained in a single verse from the Psalms: "For he is our God; and we are the people of his pasture, and the sheep of his hand" (Psalms 95:7). The relationship is simple: human submission to divine authority. And on this, the entirety of religion is based.

The psalmist's verse rests in a pastoral imagery to convey both literary and religious meaning. It is an imagery that counts for a significant amount of the thought and beauty contained in Scripture. The symbolic value of sheep in these sacred writings is unparalleled by any other beast of Creation. It is the one animal that most perfectly characterizes man's relation to God in monotheistic religion. The sheep is a flexible symbol which rings true through a continuous succession of metaphors from Genesis to Revelation.

The sheep is introduced early in the Bible: "And Abel was a keeper of sheep" (Genesis 4:2), suggesting that the relationship between the woolly beast and man goes back a long time. Anthropologists believe sheep were domesticated in the Middle Stone Age, perhaps ten thousand years ago.

The very existence of the early Hebrew tribes was dependent on sheep; the sheep that provided foods of meat and milk, and that also provided shelter, leather, and wool. The Pentateuch also attests to the role played by the sheep in the early Hebrew religious rituals. While surrounding tribes still practiced human sacrifice to the gods they considered part of the natural world, the Hebrews rested their faith in a supernatural God—an abstract God that understood the validity of vicarious sacrifice. Thus, elaborate and technical rules were drafted to ensure that the spiritual fidelity of the vicarious sacrifice was as

close to perfect as possible. And the animal most frequently chosen for this sacrifice was the sheep: "And he shall offer his offering unto the Lord, one he lamb of the first year without blemish for a burnt offering, and one ewe lamb of the first year without blemish for a sin offering, and one ram without blemish for peace offerings" (Numbers 6:14).

It was a sheep that was assigned the vital role in a biblical episode demonstrating the compassion of God for those who set absolute faith in divine command. Abraham was preparing to offer the life of his son in sacrifice to the command of God, but God, seeing Abraham's perfect fidelity, offered compassion and rescinded the command: "And Abraham lifted up his eyes, and looked, and behold behind him a ram caught in a thicket by his horns: and Abraham went and took the ram, and offered him up for a burnt offering in the stead of his son" (Genesis 22:13).

A curious, trilateral relationship was developing between God, man, and sheep. Gradually, sheep became synonymous with man, in a figurative sense, before the eyes of God and man alike. Thus, the sheep increasingly became a metaphoric entity in Scripture, representing the society of man, its helplessness and need of perpetual guidance.

The Israelite tribes saw this clearly, for they were a pastoral people. As their sheep needed the protection of a vigilant shepherd to save them from both predators and their own foolishness, so man needed the protection of a vigilant God to save him from a hostile world as well as his own human frailties: "And he said, I saw all Israel scattered upon the hills, as sheep that have not a shepherd: and the Lord said, These have no master: let them return every man to his house in peace" (I Kings 22:17).

The allegoric relationship between man and sheep is seen in its most profound simplicity in the Twenty-third Psalm: "The Lord is my shepherd; I shall not want. He maketh me to lie down in green pastures: he leadeth me beside the still waters" (Psalms 23:1–2). As the placidness of green pastures and still waters calms the sensitive sheep, so the security of divine compassion and revelation ease the fearful mind of man.

The psalm continues in its bucolic grace, extending the metaphor to where pastoral imagery symbolizes the anxiety of perdition and the guidance and command of God: "He restoreth my soul: he leadeth me in the paths of righteousness for his name's sake. Yea, though I walk through the valley of the shadow of death, I will fear no evil: for thou art with me; thy rod and thy staff they comfort me" (Psalms 23:3–4).

Since man is a social animal, there is also a need for earthly, or political, leadership, and these human leaders likewise became compared to shepherds tending the flocks of mankind. When human guidance leads the social flock astray, it is the job of the prophet to broadcast a warning: "And the word of the Lord came unto me, saying, Son of man, prophesy against the shepherds of Israel, prophesy, and say unto them, Thus saith the Lord God unto the shepherds; Woe be to the shepherds of Israel that do feed themselves! should not the shepherds feed the flocks? Ye eat the fat, and ye clothe you with the wool, ye kill them that are fed: but ye feed not the flock" (Ezekiel 34:1–3).

The metaphor extends through the entire chapter revealing a divine promise of discipline for the greedy, self-seeking shepherds and justice for the long-suffering flocks: "Therefore will I save my flock, and they shall no more be a prey. . . . And I will set up one shepherd over them, and he shall feed them, even my servant David; he shall feed them, and he shall be their shepherd. . . . And ye my flock, the flock of my pasture, are men, and I am your God, saith the Lord God" (Ezekiel 34:22–23, 31).

In a very real sense, several Israelites entrusted with leadership of men had previously been shepherds caring for the flocks. The patriarch Jacob had spent years tending the flocks of Laban, and the mighty David, before he took the scepter of the Jewish kingdom, held the staff of a shepherd. Moses, too, had once been a shepherd.

The Christian Testament hinges on Ezekiel's prophesy of a single shepherd being sent to gather and guide the straying flocks of Israel. Christ is established as the Good Shepherd who commissions his apostles to "go rather to the lost sheep of the house of Israel" (Matthew 10:6). The New Testament also is permeated with warnings of greedy and malevolent infiltrators: "Beware of false prophets, which come to you in sheep's clothing, but inwardly they are ravening wolves" (Matthew 7:15).

Sheep figure strongly in the metaphors of Christian Scripture which are told as allegoric parables to demonstrate particular points of Christian philosophy. Thus, there are episodes such as the one describing the happiness of recovering lost sheep: "What man of you, having an hundred sheep, if he lose one of them, doth not leave the ninety and nine in the wilderness, and go after that which is lost, until he find it? And when he hath found it, he layeth it on his shoulders, rejoicing. . . . I say unto you, that likewise joy shall be in heaven over one sinner that repenteth, more than over ninety and nine just persons, which need no repentance" (Luke 15:4–5, 7).

An essential significance of the sheep in Christian Scripture is found in the Revelation of St. John the Divine and the Gospel according to St. John. Here we find passages that equate Christ and the Lamb: "Behold the Lamb of God, which taketh away the sin of the world" (John 1:29). It is the mystical philosophy in which the lamb is the shepherd: "I am the good shepherd, and know my sheep, and am known of mine. As the Father knoweth me, even so know I the Father: and I lay down my life for the sheep" (John 10:14–15).

Until this point, Christian Scripture assumes the traditions and prophesies of Judaic Scripture. However, there follows a significant break. While the Israelites considered themselves the single chosen people among the world of diverse tribes, Christian prophesy is extended to the entirety of mankind: "And other sheep I have, which are not of this fold: them also I must bring, and they shall hear my voice; and there shall be one fold, and one shepherd" (John 10:16).

The Christ-Lamb metaphor reaches its ultimate mysticism in the Christian apocalypse where the Lamb (Christ) opens the seals of the book of judgment and releases the forces that destroy the physical universe. All then that remains is the glory of the spiritual universe, and its capital in the New Jerusalem: "And the city had no need of the sun, neither of the moon, to shine in it: for the glory of God did lighten it, and the Lamb is the light thereof" (Revelation 21:23).

The light of God, in this Christian vision, is seen via the faculty of Christ the Lamb. The enlightenment of the kingdom of God flows continuously through eternity: "And he shewed me a pure river of water of life, clear as crystal, proceeding out of the throne of God and of the Lamb" (Revelation 22:1).

The Christian Testament ends here, with the lamb as the image of Christ. The gentle, trusting, and innocent lamb has evolved from a dumb creature, easily led astray, to the seat of all wisdom; from the meek, sacrificial offering to the voice of ultimate authority.

Sheep have been consistent inhabitants of biblical lands ever since prehistory. The fat-tailed, domestic sheep (*Ovis aries platura*) common in the Middle East today is a species well adapted to the arid regions used for grazing. Of particular interest is its massive tail, which, after a rich spring feeding, may weigh as much as twenty pounds. This fatty tail serves as a food store and the animal may draw energy from it, much the same way a camel draws strength from its fatty hump, during the lean days of summer when the torrid sun burns away the springtime's greenery.

Also of note are the Bedouin shepherds, nomadic tribes that today tend their flocks with the traditional symbiosis that has been unchanged for more than thirty centuries.

SPIDERS

". . . as the likeness of the spider" (SURAH 29: AL 'ANKABUT:41)

THERE is something insidious about a web, that silent trap so frail, yet so lethal. And there is an element of treacherous subtlety about the architect of that web—the spider.

Predictably, the spider (order Araneae) does not occupy a spot of high acclaim in Scripture. At best, a proverb calls it "exceedingly wise," explaining, "The spider taketh hold with her hands, and is in kings' palaces" (Proverbs 30:28). But even this compliment and regal identification gives an aura of intrigue. A certain wisdom is seen in stealth. Furthermore, the identification may be in error, for the word used in the original Hebrew text, *smamit*, is not universally accepted as meaning a spider, and some scholars suspect that the writer actually meant a lizard.

More often, the spider and its web are looked upon as an evil companionship, immersed in perfidious villainy. Job described the hypocrite's rejection of God and his own false faith as a self-made trap: "Whose hope [the hypocrite's] shall be cut off, and whose trust shall be a spider's web. He shall lean upon his house, but it shall not stand: he shall hold it fast, but it shall not endure" (Job 8:14–15).

The Koran adopts the same theme: "The likeness of those who choose other patrons than Allah is as the likeness of the spider when she taketh unto herself a house, and lo! the frailest of all houses is the spider's house, if they only knew" (Surah 29: Al 'Ankabut:41).

If they only knew, they would see that the silken frailty of the web is a fatal trap. This nearly transparent web offered Isaiah a new direction for the theme. Condemning the violent, mischievous sinners, the prophet said they "weave the spider's

web. . . . Their webs shall not become garments, neither shall they cover themselves with their works: their works are works of iniquity, and the act of violence is in their hands" (Isaiah 59:5–6). The sinner cannot hide behind his misdeeds any more than a spider can hide within its slender threads.

The story of Samson and Delilah can be understood through the repugnant metaphor of spiders plotting an intrigue. It is filled with many allusions to the spider's terrible trap: "And Delilah said unto Samson, Hitherto thou hast mocked me, and told me lies: tell me wherewith thou mightest be bound. And he said unto her, If thou weavest the seven locks of my head with the web" (Judges 16:13).

Delilah, acting with all the sinister diligence of a plotting spider, waited for Samson to fall asleep, and then she set the trap, weaving the mighty Samson's hair into a web.

When Samson awoke, he realized that he was ensnared, and, with a mighty burst of energy, he broke himself free. And here we might find the literary root of the adage "One cannot trap a spider in hs own web."

Eventually, Delilah did find the source of Samson's strength—his hair. She also learned that just as the spider is defenseless without its web, so Samson would lose his strength if he was deprived of his locks. Hence, she waited until the proper opportunity, when Samson was asleep, and shaved his head, leaving not a single hair. With this intrigue surely done, she called her henchmen, the notorious Philistines, and delivered a powerless Samson into their hands.

But neither the story nor the metaphor ends here. When a spider's web is destroyed, it is still capable of building a new one. While Samson was held captive by the Philistines, his hair began to grow back and he gained strength, just as a spider spinning a new web. Chained to the stronghold of his enemies, Samson realized his strength was returning, and so started devising his last and ultimate trap.

The Israelite leader waited until a great many of his enemies were inside a very large building, and all the stones of that building became an extension of his web. Using all his strength, Samson fought against a giant pillar that supported a corner of the building and dislodged it. The ensuing collapse brought down the entire structure, killing Samson and three thousand Philistines who had tormented him.

Delilah and the Philistines had not learned all the lessons of the industrious and cunning spider. Surely, the spider's web is frail, but used properly, it is amazingly strong and versatile. Formed from a fluid manufactured within the spider's body that hardens on exposure to air, the web is woven in geometric patterns that are only now being understood by science. Within this supposedly frail construction, modern technology is finding a resiliency that spiders have known, by instinct, for millions of years.

In the Bible almost all of the numerous varieties of spiders are denoted by a single noun, *akbish*, which gives the little eight-legged creature a name that means "agile weaver."

STORKS (HERONS; EGRETS)

". . . for they had wings like the wings of a stork" (ZECHARIAH 5:9)

EVEN THE MOST NOVICE of amateur naturalists could not help but notice the remarkable affection shared between parents and offspring among the storks. Living as a close-knit family, their fond devotion and gentle ways are superb examples of wildlife living in peace with nature. There can be little wonder that mythmakers, attempting to explain the appearance of new babies to young children, chose the stork to make the delivery.

Such tender characteristics of this large and graceful bird were noticed centuries ago, even before Moses led his people to the Promised Land. Back in those days of remote antiquity, the ancient Hebrews named this bird *chasidah*, which means "pious."

In those days, the Hebrew tribes labeled the stork, and its frequent companions, the herons and egrets, as "unclean"

meat (Leviticus 11:19 and Deuteronomy 14:18). But one can't help but wonder if those Hebrews truly thought the stork unclean, or if they thought it too beautiful a bird to harm. Could these parts of the Law of Moses actually be one of man's first protected species laws?

There is also another possibility for calling the stork unclean. In nearby Egypt the subjects of pharaoh worshiped the sacred ibis, a close relative of the stork. Perhaps the Hebrews, building their early monotheistic culture despite strong outside pressures, wanted to discourage any possibility of their members from slipping into idol and animal worship. Thus, they may have taken good warning from the example of their Egyptian neighbors and branded the stork as being unclean. So to this day, we are still faced with the paradox of a most beautiful bird being recognized as "pious" and "unclean" within the

same verse of the Bible.

Today, the white stork (*Ciconia ciconia*) migrates over the land of Israel twice yearly, as it has for centuries, shuttling between European and Asian summers and African winters. Israel is particularly blessed as a focal point of these migrations because it is the only land bridge between Eurasia and Africa where migratory birds can find fresh water and food during their journeys. If they flew a bit to the west, they'd be faced with long stretches of flight over the Mediterranean Sea. If they flew to the east, their passage would be just as difficult with many miles to cover over the arid and barren Arabian peninsula.

The writers of Scripture noticed the periodic migrations and sometimes pondered the phenomenal instincts that impelled many of the beasts of creation—and not just migratory instincts, but mating, nest building, and the benevolent care of a brood of chicks. The prophet Jeremiah considered these strong instincts and observed: "Yea, the stork in the heaven knoweth her appointed times" (Jeremiah 8:7).

While most of the storks seen through the lands of the Bible are only transients, migrants on their way to distant lands, a few have always dropped out of the main flocks and built their nests in Israel, bringing an added beauty to an appealing land. Of this, the psalmist sang: "The trees of the Lord are full of sap; the cedars of Lebanon, which he hath planted; Where the birds make their nests: as for the stork, the fir trees are her house" (Psalms 104:16–17).

And as they had dozens of centuries ago, storks can still be found nesting not far from the cedars of Lebanon. One of the most popular stork nesting sites is in the Hulah Valley, that protected vale of the Upper Galilee that lies between the mountains of Lebanon and the Golan Heights. Here the white stork lives quietly in the shallow marshes and swamps at the headwaters of the Jordan River, striding with a patrician grace through growths of papyrus and water lilies. Wading through this nearly pristine environment, the stork's pure-white plumage and ebony-white wing tips add an interesting and spectacular contrast to the richly colored plants and animals of this semitropical wetland.

And where there are storks, there are likely to be herons and egrets. In fact, one normally notices these improbable neighbors of the stork first, since they are quite the opposite in temperament.

The ancient Hebrews gave a generic name to the several species of herons and egrets that inhabit the area, lumping them all together under the name *anafah*. And if the "pious" of the stork's Hebrew name seems accurate in identifying that stately bird, so is the *anafah* in describing its egret and heron neighbors. *Anafah* stems from a verb that means "anger." Gregarious and noisy birds, these *anafah* seem to be constantly bickering, fighting constantly for better places in the flock's pecking order.

Yet, somehow, these varied birds maintain a balance, and a certain tranquillity, in nature. The storks stand quietly aloof while the herons and egrets throb with an incessant, agitated murmur. And this is all part of their element, something they have lived with for uncounted ages. Despite the apparent upset that constantly has the wetland full of activity, this is really its time of peace; this is the time when life goes on according to the time-worn traditions of Creation. The flocks only truly become upset when an intruder, such as man, enters the scene. Then the birds take to wing for a short but glorious display of wonder of flight. When they are gone, the intruder senses the peace of the wetland, but it is a peace without life, which really makes it no peace at all.

The glory of a water bird's flight is, however, one of the most magnificent sights of the natural world. The stork, in particular, has a flight that is at once both powerful and graceful, and so it fits well as an image in the words of a prophet: "Then lifted I up mine eyes, and looked, and, behold, there came out two women, and the wind was in their wings; for they had wings like the wings of a stork: and they lifted up the ephah between the earth and the heaven" (Zechariah 5:9).

SWINE

"And the swine . . . is unclean to you" (LEVITICUS 11:7)

THE SWINE (*Sus scrofa*) is the symbol of filth. More than any other beast of creation, it is despised. Its unsavory reputation transcends religious dogma and sweeps deeply into many social and cultural patterns of human society.

Among English-speaking people, to say someone is a swine, or a pig, is to suggest a broad variety of insipid, unsociable characteristics, from greed and obstinancy to stupidity and filth. The swine's image is much the same in many other cultures and languages around the world, and the root for most of this attitude can be found in Scripture.

Mosaic law specifically banned the swine as an unclean animal: "And the swine, though he divide the hoof, and be clovenfooted, yet he cheweth not the cud; he is unclean to you. Of their flesh shall ye not eat, and their carcase shall ye not touch; they are unclean to you" (Leviticus 11:7–8).

If this message isn't clear enough, it is written again in Deuteronomy 14:8; the swine is an unclean animal, not to be eaten, not even to be touched. While there are many animals roaming biblical lands that don't fit into the cloven-foot and cud-chewing requirements of kosher law, the swine seems to be singled out as the epitome of uncleanliness. A firm conviction was set among the Hebrew tribes that this animal should be forever abjured.

The Islamic world has a similar aversion for swine. It is the only animal specifically banned as meat by the Koran: "Forbidden unto you [for food] are carrion and blood and swine-flesh" (Surah 5: Al Ma'idah:3). The Koran finds swine so repulsive that Mohammed notes that Allah transforms the worst sinners, the hypocrites, into swine (Surah 5: Al Ma'idah:60).

A somewhat parallel thought is found in the Bible as Isaiah draws a verbal portrait of the hypocrites who face damnation: "They that sanctify themselves, and purify themselves in the gardens behind one tree in the midst, eating swine's flesh, and the abomination, and the mouse, shall be consumed together, saith the Lord" (Isaiah 66:17).

While both the Bible and Koran set a religious prohibition on the swine, it is reasonable to assume that these dogmas may also be predicated on medical concerns. We must remember that both the ancient Hebrews and Moslems were desert peoples, inhabiting a torrid and barren wilderness. And it is exactly a torrid and barren environment that makes pork an extremely dangerous meat.

First, the intense heat of the Middle Eastern deserts tends to cause fresh meats to spoil quickly, and pork is apt to spoil more quickly than any other.

But more important is the barrenness of the area. There is not much firewood in the desert, and more than any other meat, pork must be well cooked. The reason for this is a small, wormlike parasite called trichinae that infests pork. When the meat is well cooked, these parasites are killed and pose no threat to the human who eats them. But in the middle of a desert, where wood for cooking fuel is scarce, a cook might not be able to do a thorough cooking job and leave some of the meat a little rare. In a nomadic society without the benefit of modern medicine and hospitals, eating undercooked, trichinae-infested pork could be fatal.

So it appears the best means of avoiding the deadly trichinae is to avoid pork completely. This is precisely the course followed by Jews and Moslems.

Mainstream Christian theology did not adapt this ban on swine, or any other food for that matter. Those Christians who did not live by the Old Testament injunctions involving the dietary laws leaned towards indifference on the subject. New Testament thought tended to be spiritually abstract and held an ascetic disdain for the physical world; concepts of clean and unclean should be matters of the mind, and not matters of the supper table. "There is nothing from without a man, that entering into him can defile him" (Mark 7:13).

Since both Jews and Moslems are forbidden pork, there are very few domestic pigs in the Middle East. Those that do exist are usually kept by Christians in the Christian areas of Lebanon and Israel. There are, however, considerable numbers of wild swine in the area, as both Jews and Moslems refuse to hunt them. Since there are very few natural predators for these swine, their numbers pose a constant problem, particularly to the agriculture in the area. This was also a major problem three thousand years ago when Asaph composed a psalm: "The boar out of the wood doth waste it, and the wild beast of the field doth devour it" (Psalms 80:13).

All these scriptural passages joint to make the swine a despicable animal. When a writer of Scripture wanted to use an image to convey an idea of opprobrium, he had only to turn to the swine, as in: "As a jewel of gold in a swine's snout, so is a fair woman which is without discretion" (Proverbs 11:22).

There is no mention in Scripture of the wild pig's ferocity, a characteristic well respected by experienced woodsmen and naturalists. Wild boars in particular can prove to be tough and persistent antagonists with unpredictable temperaments. They are very quick and tenacious in their attacks, and are capable of delivering serious wounds with their sharp tusks.

Contrary to some popular images, pigs are relatively clean animals, and among mammals, they are unusually intelligent.

WILD ASSES

"And the wild asses did stand in the high places" (JEREMIAH 14:6)

T HE WILD ASS has an unrestrained freedom. An untamed species, the wild ass is a perfect image of unbridled, absolute independence. Refusing the harness, it is free to roam with anarchic liberty wherever its instincts guide it.

At once, this wild freedom is an inspiration for the oppressed, and a nightmare for the status quo. We find both of these attitudes in Scripture.

Job viewed the freedom of the wild ass as a glorious quality. It is the vision of a splendid beast living within the manifold beauties of God's natural creation. It is a song that chides the imperfect constructions of man—social structures and cramped cities—and praises the boundless grandeur of divine creation: "Who hath sent out the wild ass free? or who hath loosed the bands of the wild ass? Whose house I have

made the wilderness, and the barren land his dwellings. He scorneth the multitude of the city, neither regardeth he the crying of the driver. The range of the mountains is his pasture, and he searcheth after every green thing" (Job 39:5–8).

Those creatures that avoid the hand of man will always find nourishment at the hand of God: "He sendeth the springs into the valleys, which run among the hills. They give drink to every beast of the field: the wild asses quench their thirst" (Psalms 104:10–11).

It is particularly suitable that the psalmist chose the wild ass as the animal to water at the divine springs because among all wild beasts, the wild ass undoubtedly has the most intense thirst. Capable of roaming the desert for days without a drink of water, the wild ass can withstand extreme emaciation and dehydration. When water is found, the ass can drink its fill, up-

wards of one quarter of its own weight, to restore its health. In most cases, a wild ass that has suffered severe dehydration can drink more than one hundred pounds of water at a time.

But even wild asses suffer in times of drought. Their great thirst becomes a metaphor for sinners thirsting after salvation: "And the wild asses did stand in the high places, they snuffed up the wind like dragons [jackals]; their eyes did fail, because there was no grass" (Jeremiah 14:6).

Although the unrestricted freedom of the wild ass is often used as the image of a pure independence, it is more often considered in the reverse. Complete freedom is license, it is the rejection of social structures, and he who rejects society is rejected by society.

Jeremiah castigates the followers of the pagan god Baal, comparing them to lusty wild asses in heat: "A wild ass used to the wilderness, that snuffeth up the wind at her pleasure; in her occasion who can turn her away? all they that seek her will not weary themselves; in her month they shall find her" (Jeremiah 2:24).

Job uses a similar metaphor in his reprobation of the hypocrites who know the truth of God but refuse to live by it: "Behold, as wild asses in the desert, go they forth to their work; rising betimes for a prey: the wilderness yieldeth food for them and for their children" (Job 24:5).

In each of these cases, the wilderness is the symbol for the bane of civilization, the barren wasteland that lies uncultivated by either the hand of man or the word of God. And the wild ass, which finds a tolerable home in this wilderness, becomes the symbol of the outcast.

One of the better known outcasts of Scripture was Ishmael, son of Abraham. His story is one of violence that continues to this day in the genealogical partisanship which divides Arabs and Israelis. Both trace their ancestry to Abraham, but the Moslems claim descendancy through Ishmael while the Jews claim the parentage of Isaac.

An angel of God came to announce the birth of Ishmael to Abraham's concubine Hagar with a frightening proclamation. In the original Hebrew text there is an interesting phrase in this proclamation, *pere' adom*, literally "wild ass man," which was somewhat diluted in the English translation. The angel foretells of conflict with the future outcast: "And he will be a wild man [*pere' adom*]; his hand will be against every man, and every man's hand against him" (Genesis 16:12). Ishmael is fated before birth to be a pariah.

Thus the identification of Ishmael with the wild ass is to seal his fate as an outcast. Another outcast was Nebuchadnezzar, the once mighty monarch of the Chaldeans who carried the Israelites into the Babylonian captivity. Deposed from his throne, Daniel records that the exiled King "was driven from the sons of men; and his heart was made like the beasts, and his dwelling was with the wild asses" (Daniel 5:21).

Whether the freedom of the wild ass is to be either envied or feared is a matter of conjecture. All we can be sure of is that man really didn't care very much at all for the wild ass of Scripture. The species that roamed the deserts of biblical lands for so many millenniums is today extinct. It was the Syrian wild ass (*Equus hemionus hemippus*), a diminutive creature said to be the smallest member of the horse family to inhabit the earth during historical times. It stood a bare three feet at the withers. Its meat was said to be rather tasty, and its hide a fine material for leather. As most species that have vanished during the twentieth century, the extermination of the Syrian wild ass cannot be attributed to "natural causes." It was an intelligent, cautious, and swift species, but not intelligent enough to outwit humans armed with long-range, high-powered rifles.

Although it is unlikely, some traditions claim that it was a Syrian wild ass that Jesus Christ used during his triumphant entry into Jerusalem on Palm Sunday.

The last member of this species was slaughtered in the Middle Eastern desert slightly less than a half century ago.

Another species, the Somali wild ass (*Equus africanum somaliensis*), is the Syrian wild ass' closest living relative. Its introduction to a Negev reserve stands as the only captive breeding herd on earth. There are 13 of these animals in zoos around the world, and an estimated 500 remaining in the wild near the war-torn Somali-Ethiopian border. Slightly larger than the Syrian, the Somali wild ass is also known for its swiftness. It can sustain a trot of 25 miles per hour and sprint up to about 35 miles per hour for periods of about 10 minutes. It has an amazing ability of finding food in the most barren desert areas, it can take an occasional sip of salt water in emergencies, and it is extremely wary of human beings.

The onager, or Persian wild ass (*Equus hemionus onager*), is another species of wild ass that lived in the Holy Land during the days of Scripture. In 1919, 19 onagers were introduced to the Negev where, under protection, their number has grown to 32. Attempts are being made in a few conservation circles to preserve this species, and today it is only a question of time whether the last significant wild herd, in the Badkyhz reserve of the southern Soviet Union, will survive until other breeding herds are established in more varied locales. A few other species of wild ass also survive today, and each is considered endangered. In each case, the endangerment is caused by man.

The words of Job seem ironic. If the wild ass had a spokesman, he might petition for a revision in Scripture to change an apparently unjust comparison: "For vain man would be wise, though man be born like a wild ass's colt" (Job 11:12).

WOLVES

"Benjamin shall ravin as a wolf" (GENESIS 49:27)

THE CLASSICAL IMAGE of the wolf (*Canis lupus*) as an unscrupulous plunderer is established in Scripture and enhanced through centuries of folklore and literature.

The tribe of Benjamin, destined to fulfill a role of violent treachery, was assigned the symbol of the wolf: "Benjamin shall ravin as a wolf: in the morning he shall devour the prey, and at night he shall divide the spoil" (Genesis 49:27).

The prophets seized this image and intensified it through the rest of Scripture. Denouncing the hypocrites, Jeremiah prophesized: "and a wolf of the evenings shall spoil them" (Jeremiah 5:6).

The enemies of Israel were likened to wolves, and the Chaldean cavalry was considered "more fierce than the evening wolves" (Habakkuk 1:8). Through many of these passages, we may also notice that the Israelites recognized the nocturnal habits of the wolf.

Calling for judgment on the corrupt government of Jerusalem, the prophet Ezekiel declared, "Her princes in the midst thereof are like wolves ravening the prey, to shed blood, and to destroy souls, to get dishonest gain" (Ezekiel 22:27).

Delivering the eloquent Sermon on the Mount, Christ warned his multitude of followers: "Beware of false prophets, which come to you in sheep's clothing, but inwardly they are ravening wolves" (Matthew 7:15).

Christian Scripture further fabricates this villainous image for the wolf by using it as a symbol for the more hostile members of human society. Alone with his twelve apostles, Christ charged them to preach to the world, but warned: "Go your ways: behold, I send you forth as lambs among wolves" (Luke 10:3).

The image of the wolf as the despised marauder is also found in Islamic Scripture. Recounting the deception used by the sons of Jacob when they sold their brother Joseph into slavery, the Koran says: "O our father! We went racing one with another and left Joseph by our things, and the wolf devoured him" (Surah 12: Yusuf:17).

The reason why the wolf developed this wicked image may lie in its defiance of domestication. In the wild, the wolf has dietary habits almost identical to many other carnivores, but most of the other species seem to have some redeeming qualities. Dogs, the wolf's closest relative, have accepted domestication and alliance with man, and so have the small cats. Other carnivores fulfill other functions, as food and leather sources, for beautiful furs, or even for their natural beauty.

But the wolf has none of this to offer. Rarely seen because of its preference to prowl at night, the wolf is hardly an animal of great physical beauty. In the wild, it is normally gaunt and frequently affected by mange. It is an occasional nuisance, and will snatch small livestock when it can. But more important, this wild brother of the domestic dog simply rejects domestic life, and, as in most cases where society is rejected, the defier is damned.

Today, wolves are still found in the lands of Scripture. One variety in particular, the Arabian desert wolf, is of special interest. Well adapted for hot and dry climates, the Arabian wolf is of tawny color, blending well with the desert landscape. Like all members of the wolf family, the Arabian has an extremely refined sense of hearing, extraordinary eyesight, and remarkably acute sense of smell. It also has paws that are well suited for travel over loose desert sands. These paws are relatively broad, leaving tracks that would suggest a much larger animal, and they are well insulated by thick pads that both distribute heat and absorb the shock of sharp desert gravel.

Zoologists are also making a close study of communications within the wolf family. For centuries, man has suspected that there is much sense in the barking and howling of wolves in the wild, but only recently are we learning to understand how sophisticated this communication is. There is evidence that communication among wolves is more than vocal, but also extends to facial expressions that are made and understood among members of the family.

Zoologists have also made another recent and striking discovery. Wolves possess brains that are proportionately larger in their bodies than the brain of any dog, and this is usually considered a critical factor when comparing intelligence among species. This, of course, leaves us with some interesting questions. Since dogs are direct descendants of wolves, do these findings suggest that the more intelligent members of the wolf family avoided domestication, while the more stupid members stepped into the collar and leash? Or, could it be that dogs, which were domesticated in the Middle East hundreds of centuries ago, degenerated in intelligence after their contact with man? Both questions suggest answers that may be directly opposed to the generally accepted theories of Charles Darwin.

Today, wolves are in serious trouble all over the world. Although they have been hunted for centuries, it is only the twentieth century that has brought the most sophisticated means of killing them. High-powered rifles, aircraft and rough-terrain vehicles, new poisons, massive construction and destruction of habitat, and, of course, an age-old hatred the human community has held for wolves, have all contributed to the destruction of the animal.

There is a current concern for several wolves believed to be living in the Edomite mountains of southwestern Jordan. They apparently spend the hottest part of the day in the mountains, sleeping in cool caves among the ancient cliffs. At night, they slip down the slopes and cross into Israel's Negev in search of food. This activity brings them to cross a tense and well-guarded border, contributing to the risks set on the wolf in the modern world.

Also, one of the parts of the Negev prowled by the wolves is the vast Hai Bar reserve, where several extremely rare species, such as the Dorcas gazelle and the Arabian oryx, are being bred with hopes of removing them from the endangered species list. When a desert wolf, following its instincts and normal patterns, takes one of these endangered animals for food, the damage is irreparable. And so, the wolves are hated for this too.

The wolf, most naturalists agree, has been maligned far beyond reason in most of the world. Normally, it is a rather timid animal and traditionally has served to help maintain the ecological balance of the world's wildlife. Its scavenging removes potentially hazardous carrion, and its tendency toward attacking the weaker members of any wildlife herd helps ensure that the herd as a whole remains healthy.

But society at large tends to ignore the beneficial aspects of the wolf and concentrates on the macabre image formed in Scripture and folklore. The cherished peaceable kingdom where Isaiah prophesized, "The wolf also shall dwell with the lamb" (Isaiah 11:6), is still far into the future, particularly in the attitude of man.

Even our vocabulary is tainted with a prejudicial image of *Canis lupus*. It is the vocabulary where the infinitive "to wolf" means "to devour greedily." This is not much better than the *ze'ev* that the ancient Hebrews used as a name for the animal. It stems from the verb *za'az*—"to terrify." Wolves are not greedy; indeed, they kill only what they need to live. Wolves are not really terrifying; rather, they are usually very shy and run at the sight of a man. It is man who is greedy, and man who is terrifying.

Still, one dictionary definition of a wolf is "a cruelly rapacious person." Another is "a man who makes direct amorous advances to many women." But the wolf is not inordinately predatory, and it leads an exemplary family life, being extremely devoted to its mate and offspring. The next time someone tells you "the wolf is at the door" you better hope it's a real wolf, because if it's a man with the characteristics we attribute to the wolf, you'll be in much greater danger.

Ironically, the image of the predacious wolf created in Scripture has a certain mythological accuracy. Both the ancient Jewish state and early Christian communities suffered terribly under the yoke of Roman invasion and occupation. And it must be remembered that Rome, in mythology, was founded by Romulus and Remus, stepsons of a she-wolf.

There is one note of encouragement concerning wolf

preservation in the Holy Land. Recent Israeli efforts to foster the growth of its wildlife populations have also encouraged the wolf population. Recent estimates by naturalists suggest that there are between 300 and 400 wolves, sometimes roving in packs as large as 20 members, in the wilds of the biblical land. This means that there must be a very large wildlife population to sustain so many wolves. It's a good indication that the Israeli effort to restore wildlife is meeting substantial success.